ENERGY
AND MOVEMENT

Britannica Illustrated Science Library

Encyclopædia Britannica, Inc.
Chicago ■ London ■ New Delhi ■ Paris ■ Seoul ■ Sydney ■ Taipei ■ Tokyo

Britannica Illustrated Science Library

Idea and Concept of This Work: Editorial Sol 90

Project Management: Fabián Cassan

Photo Credits: Corbis

Composition and Pre-press Services: Editorial Sol 90

Translation Services and Index: Publication Services, Inc.

Britannica Illustrated Science Library Staff

Editorial
Michael Levy, *Executive Editor, Core Editorial*
John Rafferty, *Associate Editor, Earth Sciences*
William L. Hosch, *Associate Editor, Mathematics and
    Computers*
Kara Rogers, *Associate Editor, Life Sciences*
Rob Curley, *Senior Editor, Science and Technology*
David Hayes, *Special Projects Editor*

Art and Composition
Steven N. Kapusta, *Director*
Carol A. Gaines, *Composition Supervisor*
Christine McCabe, *Senior Illustrator*

Media Acquisition
Kathy Nakamura, *Manager*

Copy Department
Sylvia Wallace, *Director*
Julian Ronning, *Supervisor*

Information Management and Retrieval
Sheila Vasich, *Information Architect*

Production Control
Marilyn L. Barton

Manufacturing
Kim Gerber, *Director*

Encyclopædia Britannica, Inc.

Jacob E. Safra, *Chairman of the Board*

Jorge Aguilar-Cauz, *President*

Michael Ross, *Senior Vice President, Corporate Development*

Dale H. Hoiberg, *Senior Vice President and Editor*

Marsha Mackenzie, *Director of Production*

International Standard Book Number (set):
    978-1-59339-382-3
International Standard Book Number (volume):
    978-1-59339-387-8
Britannica Illustrated Science Library:
    Energy and Movement 2008

Printed in China

www.britannica.com

Energy and Movement

Contents

The Source of Change

ONE GIANT SOURCE OF ENERGY
Our star, the Sun, is a huge nuclear reactor where each second more than four tons of matter are transformed into energy equivalent to almost 92 billion megatons of TNT.

We use the word "energy" daily to refer to different things. We are told, for instance, that certain food does not provide sufficient energy; we are told about the exploitation of energy resources; or we are warned by the politicians about the energy crises. When we are tired, we have "no energy." We also hear about alternative sources of energy and the mention, by some religions and pseudosciences, of spiritual energy—and so on. But what is energy? In general, and in the sense used in this book, energy is "the potential to produce change," the capacity to act, transform, or set in motion. Other accepted meanings that we will use refer to energy as a natural resource and as the technology associated with exploiting and using the resource, both industrially and economically.

The development of steam engines during the Industrial Revolution generated the need for engineers to develop formulas and concepts to describe the thermal and mechanical efficiencies of the systems they were developing. Thus, they began speaking about "energy." Energy is an abstract physical quantity. This means that it cannot be measured in a pure state but that only variations of energy in material systems can be observed. These variations are equivalent to the work required to change one system from its initial state to a subsequent one. Energy cannot be created or destroyed; it can only be transformed from one form to another. Obviously there are forms of energy that can be transformed or used more easily than others and, in the end, all forms of energy will become heat energy, one of the most disordered forms of energy. This loss of energy in the form of heat results in machines and human-developed processes working with less than the 100 percent efficiency one would expect if one were to apply the principle of the conservation of energy literally.

However, as already mentioned, there is also another definition of the word "energy" that refers to the natural resources necessary to produce energy as engineers and physicists understand it. This understanding of energy is very important and affects us all. Its role in the global economy is essential, and it could be said that most recent wars have had as one of their goals the control of energy resources—both renewable and nonrenewable.

In this book, we present some of the most important sources of energy used by humanity. We show how human ingenuity has been able to put the different forms of energy at its service by developing machines of all kinds, and we describe some of the most important manifestations of energy in the natural world. We also dedicate a chapter to describe the uses of clean, renewable sources of energy, including solar, wind, water, and geothermal sources. Finally, we list some of the inventions that people throughout history have developed to satisfy their instinct to explore. These are inventions that made people move faster and travel farther with less and less energy. The progression from animal-driven transportation to steam engines and internal-combustion engines is a key to understanding modern civilization. •

Origin and Sources

Because energy can take on many forms, there are many possible sources from which we can generate both work and heat. Some of these sources, such as the Sun or the atom, are the very reasons for our existence, and it could almost be said that the other forms of energy are derived from them. Others, such as natural gas, petroleum (oil), or

AMUAY REFINERY
This petroleum refinery is one of the
largest in the world. It is located in the
state of Falcón in Venezuela.

coal, are the result of geologic processes that have taken billions of years to complete. Some of these sources are renewable, but others run the risk of being exhausted if we do not use them wisely. The truth is that we find ourselves in a time when we must rethink our habits of energy usage. ●

Sources of Energy

E nergy is vital to life. From it, we get light and heat, and it is what allows economic growth. Most of the energy we use comes from fossil fuels, such as petroleum, coal, and natural gas—substances that took millions of years to form and that will someday be depleted. For this reason, there are more and more countries investing in technologies that take advantage of clean, renewable energy from the Sun, wind, water, and even the interior of the Earth. ●

NATURAL NUCLEAR REACTOR
The solar energy absorbed by the Earth in a year is equivalent to 20 times the energy stored by all the fossil-fuel reserves in the world and 10,000 times greater than the current consumption of energy.

Nonrenewable Sources

These are the sources of energy that are limited and can forever be depleted through use. They represent up to 85 percent of the world's energy consumption and form the basis of today's insecure energy economy. These nonrenewable sources of energy can be classified into two large groups: fossil fuels (coal, petroleum, and natural gas) and nuclear energy, which is produced in nuclear power plants from uranium— a scarce, controlled radioactive material.

PRIMARY GLOBAL ENERGY SOURCES

Percentages are for the year 2003

- Petroleum **36%**
- Coal **24%**
- Renewable resources **13%**
- Nuclear energy **6%**
- Natural gas **21%**

B NUCLEAR ENERGY
One of the methods of obtaining electrical energy is through the use of controlled nuclear reaction. This technology continues to be the center of much controversy because of the deadly wastes it generates.

A FOSSIL CHEMICAL ENERGY
Fossil fuels (coal, natural gas, and petroleum) are the result of the sedimentation of plants and animals that lived millions of years ago and whose remains were deposited at the bottom of estuaries and swamps. Fossil fuels are the main source of energy for industrial societies. Their combustion releases into the atmosphere most of the gases that cause acid rain and the greenhouse effect.

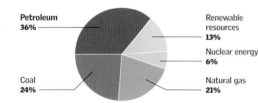

THERE COULD BE NO MORE COAL RESERVES AFTER THE YEAR

2300.

COAL
Coal drove the Industrial Revolution in the developed world. It still provides a quarter of the world's commercial energy. Coal is easy to obtain and use, but it is the dirtiest of all energy resources.

GAS MIGHT RUN OUT IN THE YEAR

2150.

NATURAL GAS
Formed by the breakdown of organic matter, it can be found in isolation or deposited together with petroleum. One way of transporting it to places of consumption is through gas pipelines.

Renewable Sources

Renewable energy resources are not used up or exhausted through use. As long as they are used wisely, these resources are unlimited because they can be recovered or regenerated. Some of these sources of energy are the Sun, the wind, and water. Depending on the form of exploitation, biomass and geothermal energy can also be considered renewable energy resources.

C HYDROELECTRIC ENERGY
is generated by turbines or water wheels turned by the fall of water. Its main drawback is that the construction of reservoirs, canals, and dams modifies the ecosystems where they are located.

D SOLAR ENERGY
The Sun provides the Earth with great quantities of energy, which can be used for heating as well as for producing electricity.

E WIND ENERGY
ultimately comes from the Sun. Solar radiation creates regions of high and low pressure that creates currents of air in the atmosphere. Wind is one of the most promising renewable energy resources, because it is relatively safe and clean.

F GEOTHERMAL ENERGY
is produced by the heat in the crust and mantle of the Earth. Its energy output is constant, but power plants built to access it must be located in places where water is very close to these heated regions.

G HYDROGEN ENERGY
The production of hydrogen is a new and, for the moment, costly process. But, unlike other fuels, hydrogen does not pollute.

H RENEWABLE CHEMICAL ENERGY BIODIGESTERS
produce fuel from biological resources, such as wood, agricultural waste, and manure. It is the primary source of energy in the developing regions. The methane gas it produces can be used for cooking or to generate electricity.

I TIDAL ENERGY
is one of the newer forms of producing electrical energy. It harnesses the energy released by the ocean as its rises and falls (the ebb and flow of tides).

J BIOFUEL ENERGY
The most common biofuels are ethanol and biodiesel, which are produced from conventional agricultural products, such as oilseeds, sugarcane, or cereals. In the future, they are expected to partially or completely replace gasoline or diesel.

PETROLEUM WILL RUN OUT IN THE YEAR
2050.

PETROLEUM
Petroleum is the most important energy resource for modern society. If it were to suddenly be depleted, it would be a catastrophe: airplanes, cars, ships, and thermal power plants, among many other things, would be inoperable.

21%
PERCENT OF "GREEN" ELECTRICITY THAT EUROPE PLANS TO USE IN 2010

Matter

The dictionary says that matter is everything that takes up space. In other words, whatever makes up a substance in the physical universe—the Earth, the seas, the Sun, the stars—is matter. Everything that humans see, touch, or feel is matter. Matter can be hard as steel, adaptable as water, and shapeless as the oxygen in the air. The study of matter has permitted the fabrication of tools, construction of cities, and even flights into space. Regardless of what is currently known about it, the more scientists look into matter, the more complexity they find. For example, it is now known that not even the hardest diamond is really solid, because the atom—the heart of matter—is almost all empty space. ●

What Is Matter Made of?

 Matter is made of small particles called atoms. The atoms group themselves and form molecules, which are arranged into the various forms of matter. In our daily lives, the most commonly recognized states in which matter exists are solid, liquid, and gas. In solid state, bodies have an almost invariable volume because their particles (atoms, ions, or molecules) are in such close contact that they can get no closer. When the temperature is high enough (melting), particles lose their fixed positions and, although they are still very close, the crystalline structures exclusive to solids disappear in changing to the liquid state. Above the boiling point, the particles lose contact with each other and move freely (gaseous state).

Gas

Solid

Liquid

SUBLIMATION

DEPOSITION

From the Solid State to the Gaseous

Ice and steam are the same substance as liquid water. The difference lies in the strength with which their molecules attract each other and the way in which they group themselves. Water molecules have the same shape and the same atoms in the three states. Water can change directly from ice to a gaseous state, but the process, called sublimation, occurs slowly at normal air pressure.

A
Solid State

As a general rule, in solids the particles (atoms or molecules) are closer together than liquids. That is why the density of a solid substance is greater than in the liquid state. However, water is an exception. In other words, when water freezes, it expands and becomes lighter. Ice floats on water because of this process. When the temperature of a piece of ice increases, the molecules increase their vibration and their separation.

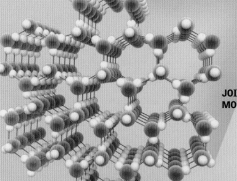

JOINED MOLECULES

32° F
(0° C)

Freezing point.
The temperature at which water passes from the liquid to solid state.

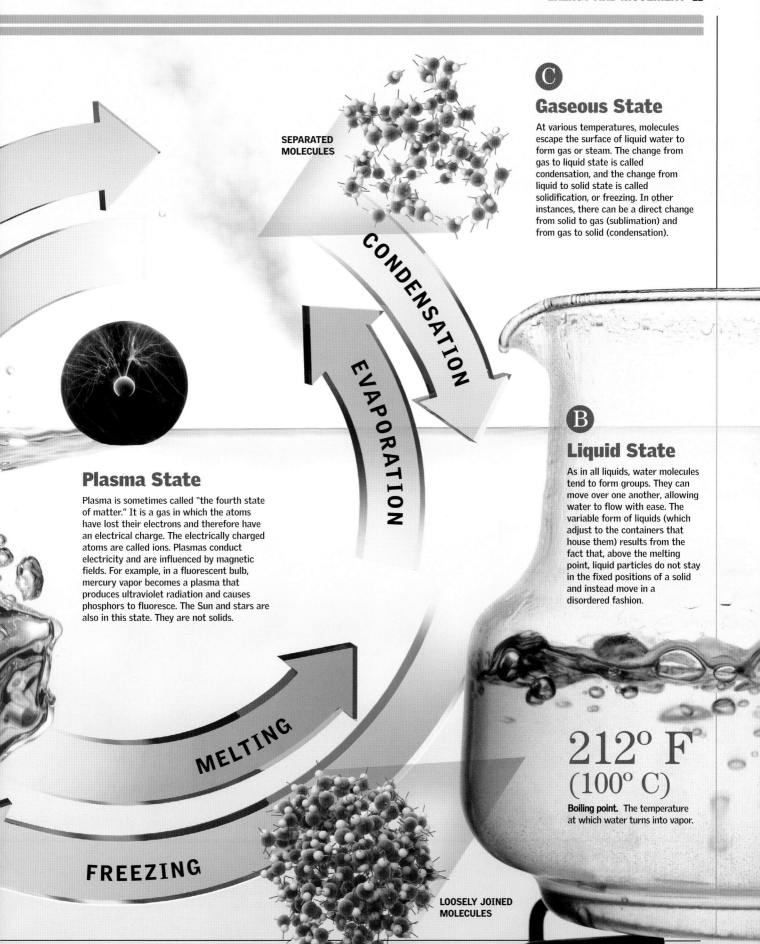

C

Gaseous State

At various temperatures, molecules escape the surface of liquid water to form gas or steam. The change from gas to liquid state is called condensation, and the change from liquid to solid state is called solidification, or freezing. In other instances, there can be a direct change from solid to gas (sublimation) and from gas to solid (condensation).

SEPARATED MOLECULES

CONDENSATION

EVAPORATION

B

Liquid State

As in all liquids, water molecules tend to form groups. They can move over one another, allowing water to flow with ease. The variable form of liquids (which adjust to the containers that house them) results from the fact that, above the melting point, liquid particles do not stay in the fixed positions of a solid and instead move in a disordered fashion.

Plasma State

Plasma is sometimes called "the fourth state of matter." It is a gas in which the atoms have lost their electrons and therefore have an electrical charge. The electrically charged atoms are called ions. Plasmas conduct electricity and are influenced by magnetic fields. For example, in a fluorescent bulb, mercury vapor becomes a plasma that produces ultraviolet radiation and causes phosphors to fluoresce. The Sun and stars are also in this state. They are not solids.

MELTING

FREEZING

212° F (100° C)

Boiling point. The temperature at which water turns into vapor.

LOOSELY JOINED MOLECULES

The Atom

I n physics and chemistry, an atom is the smallest unit of a chemical element that retains its identity and properties; it cannot be divided any further by chemical processes (it can, however, be divided by physical processes). All matter in the universe is made up of atoms. This concept originated in ancient Greece, but the existence of the atom was not demonstrated until the 19th century. The development of nuclear physics in the 20th century led to the discovery that the atom can be subdivided into various types of smaller particles.

Nucleus

determines the physical properties that distinguish one element from another. It contains most of the atom's mass (atomic weight).

PROTONS
ELECTRICAL CHARGE: POSITIVE
ATOMIC WEIGHT: 1
The quantity of protons determines the chemical element to which the atom belongs. For example, if three protons are removed from a lead atom, a gold atom remains.

NEUTRONS
ELECTRICAL CHARGE: NEUTRAL
ATOMIC WEIGHT: 1
Helps hold the nucleus together.

How It Is Held Together

Because protons have positive charges, they repel each other. However, the atomic nucleus remains intact because of another force of greater magnitude, though of shorter range, known as the strong nuclear interaction.

Protons

The electric field is **long range.**

Short-range nuclear force

The two positive electric fields repel each other.

If the protons get close enough, the nuclear force attracts them and keeps them joined.

Neutrons add nuclear force, without an electric charge, reinforcing the bond.

ISOTOPES
The nucleus of a given element can have a variable number of neutrons without changing its fundamental nature. These variations of the same element have slightly different behaviors and are known as isotopes.

RADIOACTIVITY
Certain unstable isotopes decay over time, emitting particles and radiation.

Particles

IONS

If the number of electrons is equal to the number of protons, the atom is electrically neutral.

If the atom loses an electron, it transforms into a positive ion, or cation.

If it gains an extra one, it becomes a negative ion, or anion.

History of the Atomic Theory

500 BC
ANCIENT GREECE
Democritus and Leucippus assert that matter is composed of tiny, indivisible particles that are in constant motion.

1808
JOHN DALTON
states that atoms of a same element measure and weigh the same but not those of a different element.

1869
DMITRY MENDELEYEV
organizes the elements according to their atomic weight in the so-called periodic table of elements.

Invisible to the Microscope

The atoms cannot be seen through a microscope (either optical or electronic). Computational advancements have allowed us to obtain images of the position that atoms occupy in a substance, but the structure of each individual atom has not been imaged.

ATOMIC STRUCTURE

Nucleus: The densest part of the atom

Electron cloud: Lightest region that surrounds the nucleus

Diameter 0.0000001 mm

10 trillion

THE NUMBER OF ATOMS THAT CAN FIT ON THE SURFACE OF A PINHEAD

Electron Cloud

The electrons are found in the electron cloud. An electron has a negative electrical charge and an atomic weight of 0.0005434 amu. The electrons determine the chemical and electrical properties of elements, and they are involved in bonding with other atoms. Within the electron cloud, the electrons are distributed in orbits, or orbitals.

Electron Orbitals

RUTHERFORD-BOHR MODEL (PLANETARY MODEL)
This model, which is obsolete, depicted electrons as planets that revolve around the nucleus. However, it is the model that persists in popular perception.

VALENCE SHELL MODEL (QUANTUM MODEL)
The electrons are not in a fixed orbit but in regions of greater or lesser probability, and they can move in any direction within the region.

Quantum Leap

Niels Bohr discovered that electrons orbit the atom with discrete levels or quanta of energy—that is, not all orbitals are permitted but only a finite number. The electrons jump from one level to another in quantum leaps. If a jump is from a higher energy level to a lower one, a photon is released (emits light). If the jump is reversed, a photon is captured (absorbs light).

Molecules

are typically structures with two or more atoms joined by bonds that can be covalent, or ionic.

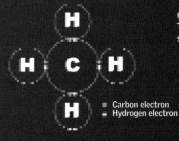

COVALENT BOND
The bonding electrons are shared by both atoms.

■ Carbon electron
■ Hydrogen electron

IONIC BOND
An electron abandons the least electronegative atom to become part of the electron cloud of the more electronegative one.

Electronic bond
■ Sodium electron
■ Chlorine electron

1911

ERNEST RUTHERFORD develops the first coherent model that explains the atomic structure. It was improved in 1913 by Niels Bohr.

1920

QUANTUM MECHANICS sets the foundation for the discovery of atoms in the 20th century. In 1932, neutrons were discovered, completing the model.

Electricity

t present, the most used form of energy is electricity. This is because of the flexibility of the existing methods used in its generation, because of the advantages of using high-voltage power lines, and because electric engines are more efficient than heat engines. The drawbacks to this form of energy stem from the fact that it is not possible to store large amounts of electricity and the fact that transmission lines are expensive. ●

The World of Electrons

ELECTRIC CHARGE
An atom that loses or gains an electron is called an ion and becomes electrically charged.

POSITIVE ION
Atom lacking one or more electrons

NEGATIVE ION
Atom with one or more extra electrons

CIRCUIT
By joining two objects of opposite charges with a conductor, an electrical circuit is formed.

NEGATIVE TERMINAL
(excess electrons)

POSITIVE TERMINAL
(missing electrons)

CONDUCTOR
transports the electrons from the negative pole to the positive one.

CONVENTIONAL CURRENT
Current flows from the positive terminal to the negative one

COMPASS

The compass needle aligns with the field of the circuit.

Magnetic field.

High-voltage power lines

MAGNETISM
A magnetic field, similar to that created by a magnet, is created around a wire with an electric current. The effects of this process can be seen on a compass.

DISTRIBUTION
To carry the current, the voltage needs to be increased.

High-voltage power lines

It is cheaper to transport high-voltage current than one with low voltage.

| **GENERATOR** 16,500 volts | **TRANSFORMER** 230,000 volts | **TRANSFORMER** 220 volts | **TRANSFORMER** 13,200 volts | **HOUSEHOLD USE** 120 volts |

Industrial Production

The core of an electric power plant consists of the generators that use magnetism to produce electricity.

1 By moving a magnet across a conductor, a temporary current is produced.

2 If the magnet is moved away, the current flows in the opposite direction.

Magnet Conductor

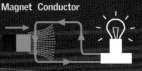

Magnet Conductor

3 By keeping the magnet moving, the current remains constant but reverses direction continuously. This type of current is called alternating current (AC).

UNITS OF MEASUREMENT

AMPERE	MAIN UNIT
VOLT	ELECTRIC POTENTIAL (VOLTAGE)
WATT	ELECTRIC POWER
OHM	ELECTRICAL RESISTANCE

How a Generator Works

1 MOTIVE FORCE
Water, steam, or wind is used depending on the type of generator.

2 TURBINE
Its blades convert the linear power into rotary power.

3 ROTATING MAGNET
The turbine constantly moves a powerful magnet.

60 CYCLES PER SECOND
Number of times that a full turn of the magnet is produced; the alternating current changes direction.

TURBINE

AXLE

MAGNET

Magnetic North Pole

Magnetic South Pole

COIL

The axle transmits the rotational motion of the magnet.

TYPES OF GENERATORS	TURBINE MOVED BY
HYDROELECTRIC	WATER
WIND	WIND
THERMOELECTRIC	FUEL
THERMONUCLEAR	NUCLEAR POWER

4 COIL
A wound conductor that is connected to the circuit

5 ELECTRICITY
The motion of the magnetic field on the coil generates an electric current.

Manifestations of Energy

P eople have always looked for ways to harness energy. The first rudimentary tools were developed so that more work could be done with less effort.

When humans abandoned tropical zones, they had to find ways of using energy to keep warm. From the development of fire-making techniques to the technology of modern nuclear

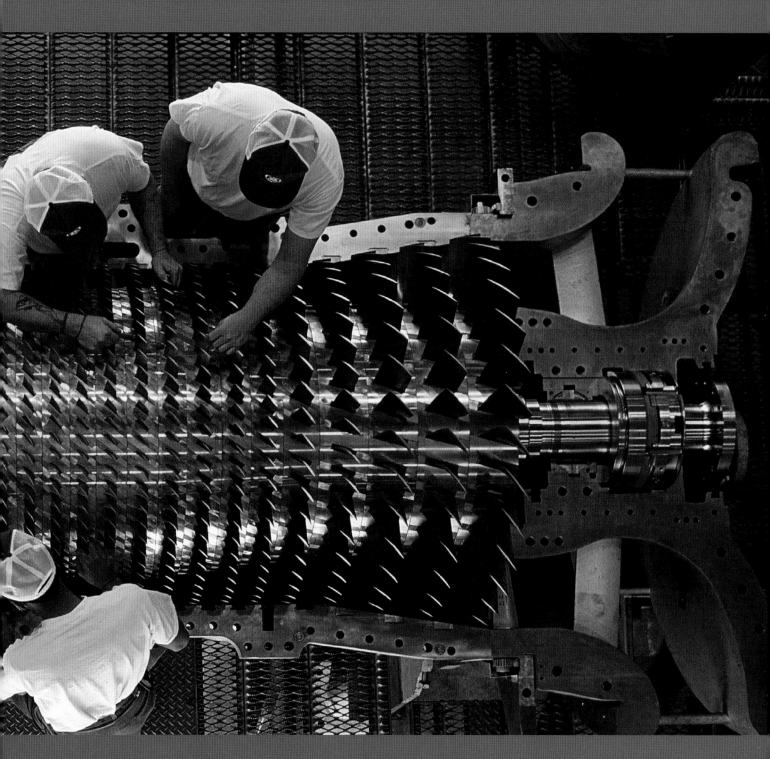

A TURBINE EVERY THREE DAYS
These workers are assembling a 38-megawatt gas turbine in a General Electric plant in South Carolina. On average, they assemble a turbine every three days.

reactors is but a small step if measured on a geologic scale. Here we present some of the machines and devices that people have invented and utilized over the course of history, from the simplest, such as the wheel or pendulum, to the most complex, such as the turbine and steam engine. ●

The Wheel

ogether with fire, the wheel is one of the key inventions in the history of humankind. It was invented in Mesopotamia, where it was successful, and it was distributed through the Old World thanks to the abundance of large beasts of burden. Pre-Columbian American culture also discovered the wheel, but did not use it to go beyond the manufacture of toys and small artifacts; this scenario arose because of the lack of large beasts of burden to facilitate the use of vehicles—and also because the most advanced civilizations did not occupy flat terrain.

The wheel permits the movement of heavy objects with less effort than dragging them over a surface.

In its basic form, the wheel is a movable disk that rotates around a fixed axle.

Axle

Disk

Tripartite Wheel

The most common type of primitive wheel. It is still used in many parts of the world and is very suitable for rough terrain.

Fenestrated
The first attempt to reduce the weight of the wheel

Tripartite
More versatile and economical than the solid wheel, it is also very resistant.

History

Solid wheel
A simple cross section of a tree trunk with a hole in its middle

STEEL RIMS
Their purpose is to reduce the wear of the wheel. They were used throughout the Middle Ages.

1 A red-hot iron hoop slightly larger than the wheel is placed over it.

2 After the metal cools, it contracts, strongly gripping the wood.

DEVELOPMENT

Sleds
Previously the cargo was placed over two wooden guides that slid across the ground.

Rollers
The cargo was moved over a bed of wooden rollers. The rollers left free at the back were placed again in front.

Solid wheels
The first wheels were simple clay disks connected by a tree trunk.

Reducing Friction

The friction of the wheel with the axle makes the movement more difficult and causes the pieces to wear out quickly.

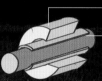

Hub

Axle

Leather bearing
Introduced by the Celts in France and Germany around 100 BC

Wooden rollers
A bed of small wooden bars that turn freely. This gave rise to modern bearings.

Wheels and Machines

The wheel transmits and transfers force.

With spokes
Ideal for fabricating very light wheels

With rims
Combines lightness with toughness

Potter's wheel
The first use of the wheel, even earlier than its use in transportation

Mills
use the force of wind or water to grind grains or pump underground water to the surface.

Gears
permit the transmission and transformation of force into speed and vice versa.

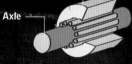

The Pendulum

T his simple machine, whose physical principle was discovered by Galileo Galilei, has had many practical applications, especially in making clocks, in which the pendulum is used to drive the clock's inner workings. A small initial impulse can generate a considerable amount of motion that, through axles and gears, can be transformed into energy. The pendulum was used in 1851 by Jean-Bernard-Léon Foucault to demonstrate both the rotation of the Earth and the Coriolis effect. ●

Foucault Pendulum

A device designed by the French physicist Jean-Bernard-Léon Foucault in 1851, which serves to demonstrate that the Earth revolves on its axis

THE EXPERIMENT
Foucault started the pendulum swinging and observed its oscillation.

The pendulum was sufficiently heavy to swing for several hours without stopping.

Little by little, the pendulum oscillated in a slightly different direction. After one day, it had made three fourths of a turn.

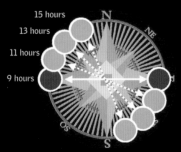

15 hours
13 hours
11 hours
9 hours

Foucault deduced that if the plane of oscillation of the pendulum cannot change, it was the Earth that revolved underneath the pendulum.

An imaginary pendulum on one of the two poles would always oscillate in the same direction.

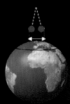

Although, if seen from Earth, it would appear to rotate around its own axis.

The same is true if the pendulum is placed on a rotating plane, as in a carousel.

The pendulum always oscillates in the same direction, even if the carousel rotates.

To an observer on the carousel, the pendulum appears to turn.

Applications

METRONOME

It is used by musicians to measure time.
The duration depends on the distance between the weight and the point of rotation. The greater the distance, the longer the oscillation period.

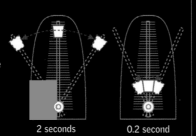

2 seconds   0.2 second

CLOCK MAKING

The first mechanical clocks used pendulums to move their hands at a constant speed.
Each oscillation takes the same amount of time.

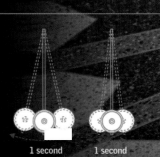

1 second   1 second

Vertical axis

Rotation point

String

String

It has a symmetric weight that hangs
from a string tied to a fixed point.

When the weight is moved from
its equilibrium point, it oscillates.

Oscillation plane
The motion remains in a
constant plane.

It stops because of air resistance
and friction on the string.

Weight

Equilibrium point

rc

Vertical axis

High-tech Models

15 m

3 m

Pendulums are
manufactured in large
sizes, providing greater
impulse and taking
longer to slow down.

CONTINUOUS MOTION
Achieved using a ring-shaped
electromagnet

STRING

RING

When the string crosses
a certain threshold, a
sensor is activated that
turns on the
electromagnet. This
process provides the
necessary impulse to
keep the pendulum from
stopping.

The Compass

This invention uses the force of the Earth's magnetic field for its operation. The compass was of fundamental importance to navigation, because it allowed sailors to orient themselves on the open sea without having to observe the stars (which cannot be seen on cloudy nights or during the day). With the development of satellite-based global positioning systems, the use of compasses has greatly declined. However, because of their versatility, low weight, and low cost, compasses still have a place in some sporting and recreational activities.

Navigation Compass

➤ The compass is used to trace a course on a navigation chart. Compasses range from simple handheld models, such as the one shown here, to complex models that were used for navigation at sea.

PIVOT
Low-friction support on which the needle sits

MAGNETIC NEEDLE
always orients itself with the Earth's magnetic north. By convention, the end that points north is colored red. More modern compasses replace the needle with a system of magnets.

BASELINE
is used to align the axis of the compass with the chosen direction.

POINTER
rotates with the graduated dial and points to the north on the dial.

GRADUATED DIAL
The rotating dial is graduated from 0 to 360° and includes the four cardinal points.

History

Magnetite, a magnetic mineral, was discovered in Magnesia, Asia Minor.

The Chinese already knew the usefulness of the magnet for navigating.

6th Century BC   1st Century AD

HOW TO FIND NORTH

The magnetized needle always points north.

The cardinal points are correctly positioned when the pointer lines up with the needle.

HOW TO FOLLOW A BEARING

Baseline

1 The compass is pointed toward the destination by aligning it with the baseline.

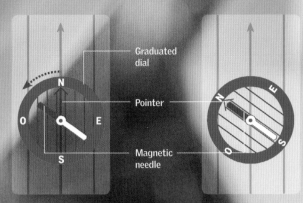

Graduated dial

Pointer

Magnetic needle

2 The graduated dial is rotated until the pointer is lined up with the magnetic needle.

3 Keeping the pointer lined up with the needle ensures that the direction is maintained.

MAGNETIC DECLINATION

MAGNETIC NORTH
does not coincide with the geographic north because the magnetic field varies with the movement of masses within the Earth.

GEOGRAPHIC NORTH

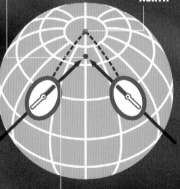

DECLINATION ANGLE
The angular difference between the magnetic and the geographic north. All navigation maps give this value to adjust for local compass readings.

THE EARTH'S MAGNETISM

1 The Earth has in its core a great mass of molten magnetic iron.

2 This turns it into a great magnet that generates a magnetic field around it.

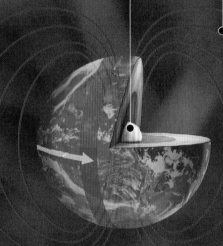

3 The magnetic needle of the compass points in a north-south direction once it lines up with the Earth's magnetic field.

Arabs bring to Europe a compass similar to that used by the Chinese.

It is used for navigating the Mediterranean Sea.

Gimbals are used to keep a compass horizontal despite movements of the ship.

It is discovered that the magnetic north does coincide with the geographic one. Magnetic declination is studied.

More precise instruments and systems, such as radar, radionavigation, and satellite navigation, are implemented.

12th century   13th century   15th century   19th century   20th century

The Steam Engine

This external combustion engine, which transforms the energy in water vapor into mechanical work, was essential to the Industrial Revolution that took place in England in the 17th and 18th centuries. The history of its invention goes back to rudimentary devices without practical application and continues up to the invention of the steam engine by James Watt. The steam engine was of fundamental importance for industry and transportation, replacing beasts of burden, the mill, and even human laborers. ●

How It Worked

1 ASCENT
The pressure of the steam makes the piston rise.

2 DESCENT
Without heat, the steam condenses, the pressure disappears, and the piston falls.

Piston
Reservoir
Steam
Water
Heat

Steam condenses
Water returns to its initial level

COMPARISON OF SOURCES OF ENERGY ABOUT 1800

WATT'S STEAM ENGINE 11 TO 30 KILOWATTS

= **14 TO 40** horses

HORSE moving a mill **300 TO 450 WATTS**

= **36.6 MEN** (minimum)

Watt's Innovation

added a separate container where the steam condenses.

1 The valves allow steam to pass through either from the top or from the bottom.

2 The piston goes up or down according to the intake of the steam.

Intake   Exhaust

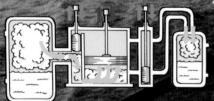

Boiler

3 The steam expelled by the motion of the piston becomes liquid in the condenser.

INNOVATOR

NAME	JAMES WATT
NATIONALITY	SCOTTISH
OCCUPATION	ENGINEER

The changes he introduced made it possible to apply the steam engine to industrial processes.

Applications of the Era
Mainly in industry, mining, and transportation

WATER EXTRACTION
Basing his design on an earlier model, Thomas Savery in 1698 patented a steam engine that was used to extract water from mines. In 1712, Thomas Newcomen perfected it.

SPINNING AND WEAVING
It was used first to create spinning and weaving machines, and it was used later in printing presses.

STERILIZATION
About 1900, this model was built. It served, among other things, to sterilize water for nursing and for preparing medications.

TRANSPORTATION
In ships, cars, and locomotives. Some locomotives, like the Rocket, reached speeds close to 36 miles per hour (58 km/h).

GENERATING ELECTRICITY
Currently this is one of the steam engine's most important uses. The steam is sent through a turbine, and its mechanical energy is transformed into electrical energy.

Dynamite

he term "dynamite" comes from the Greek word *dynamis*, which means "force." It was invented by Alfred Nobel in 1867, and it quickly replaced nitroglycerin, which was unstable and dangerous. Dynamite was the most commonly used explosive until 1950. It is so stable that new sticks in good condition generally do not explode even when exposed to fire; a detonator is necessary to make them explode. The fortune that Alfred Nobel earned with his invention was used for the creation of the award that carries his name.

How It Works

1 The detonators are connected to the sticks of dynamite. By means of a safety fuse, the detonators are attached to the central detonator.

2 When the detonator is activated, a small explosion is created, causing the subsequent explosion of the dynamite.

3 Dynamite explodes when the detonators are activated.

Safety fuse

Dynamite

1 Detonators

Exploder

WHAT IT WAS USED FOR

Blasting in mines and quarries

Tunnel construction

Demolition

Military use

What It Is Made of

3 PARTS NITROGLYCERIN

Glycerin + sulfuric acid + nitric acid

NITROGLYCERIN

Thick, oily, colorless or yellow liquid. Very volatile, sensitive to shock, friction, and heat.

+

1 PART DIATOMACEOUS EARTH (kieselguhr)

Very porous and absorbent material. When mixed with nitroglycerin, it produces a malleable paste, reducing nitroglycerin's notorious volatility.

History of Explosives

GUNPOWDER
Invented in China
Made of sulfur, carbon, and potassium nitrate. The first explosive in history, it was at first used only to shoot fireworks.

10th Century AD

NITROGLYCERIN
Ascanio Sobrero
Made with glycerol, sulfuric acid, and nitric acid. It is a very powerful explosive that is liquid and colorless. Unstable and very volatile, it explodes easily.

1846

NITROCELLULOSE
Christian Schönbein
Cellulose + nitric acid + sulfuric acid. It is known as smokeless gunpowder because it has great explosive power, but, unlike gunpowder, it does not give off black smoke.

1846

DETONATOR

The detonator, or blasting cap, is activated by lighting a fuse. It was invented by Nobel.

Crimps

Shell

Fuse

Ignition charge

Primer charge

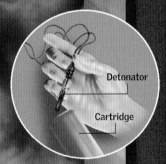

Detonator

Cartridge

SAFETY FUSE

Made up of layers of impermeable plastic that protect the gunpowder core

ELECTRIC DETONATORS

supply direct current to the detonators, permitting their activation from a great distance.

RACK

Pressure

TWIST

Turn

EXTERNAL CARTRIDGE

protects and contains the interior (dynamite). It minimizes the leaking of nitroglycerin and protects it from moisture and water.

TNT (TRINITROTOLUENE)
Joseph Wilbrand
Made of carbon, hydrogen, oxygen, and nitrogen. Potent explosive. Solid, colorless or pale yellow, and odorless. It is exploded with a detonator.

1863

DYNAMITE
Alfred Nobel
patented dynamite in 1867. He operated several factories where the explosive was produced.

1867

MODERN EXPLOSIVES
Ammonium nitrate is the basis for modern explosives. An example is ANFO, a mixture of ammonium nitrate and fuel, which is currently the most commonly used explosive.

1955

The Battery

G enerates electrical power by means of a chemical process that alters the characteristics of its components, and consequently a battery becomes discharged after a certain amount of use. The battery can produce an electric current between its two terminals, which are also known as poles or electrodes. The battery derives its name from the early practice of lining cells together horizontally, like batteries of troops. ●

Adding Together Energy

IN PARALLEL
The positive terminals are first connected to each other, followed by the negative ones.

The voltage remains the same, but the batteries last longer.

1.5 V

IN SERIES
The negative terminal of one connects to the negative terminal of the next one.

1.5 V

The voltage of the batteries is added. The power remains the same.

Two 1.5 V batteries produce 3 V.

9 V BATTERY

Formed by six 1.5 V cells in series.

1.5 V x 6 = 9 V

POSITIVE TERMINAL
has the shape of a circular button.

PLASTIC LINING
serves as insulation.

NICKEL-PLATED STEEL CASE
contains the active ingredients and is the positive collector.

OPERATION

NEGATIVE TERMINAL
produces the electrons that enter the circuit to make it work.

1 When the battery is connected to an electrical circuit, the **zinc** in the anode **oxidizes**.

2 For each zinc atom that oxidizes, two **electrons** are released.

3 A residue of very unstable **zinc ions** is left behind.

4 The anode collector conducts the electrons to the negative terminal of the cell.

5 From the **negative terminal,** the electrons enter the electrical circuit.

AA Model

Standard measurements (mm)

1.00 minimum

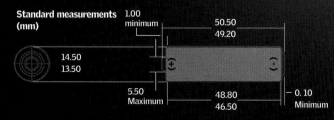

14.50
13.50

50.50
49.20

5.50 Maximum

48.80
46.50

0. 10 Minimum

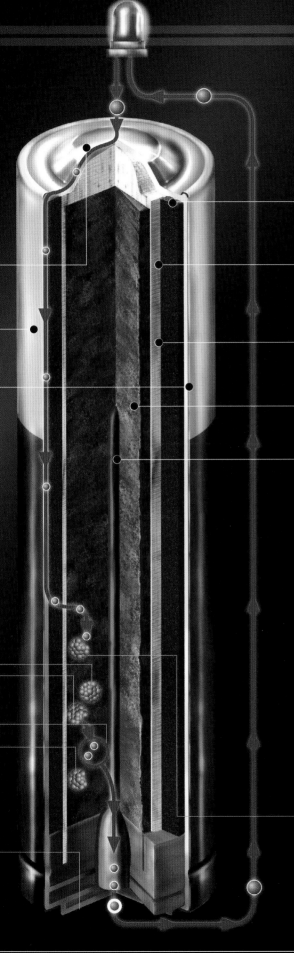

ALKALINE BATTERY

VOLTAGE	1.5 V
DURATION IN WATT-HOURS	2.5
IN AMPERE-HOURS	2.8

CATHODE
Made of manganese dioxide and graphite, it receives electrons from an external circuit.

ELECTROLYTE
A solution of potassium hydroxide that transports the ionic current inside the cell

SEPARATOR
Made of porous, nonwoven fabric. It separates the electrodes and also contains the electrolyte.

ANODE
Zinc powder. It serves as the source of electrons.

ANODE COLLECTOR
Tin-covered metal. It conducts the electrons from the anode to the external circuit.

POSITIVE TERMINAL
receives the electrons from the circuit to keep the tension high.

6 Takes up the electrons and transfers them to the cathode.

7 The electrons combine with the manganese dioxide to form negative ions.

8 These ions combine with the water in the electrolyte. They separate into negative hydroxide ions and positive hydrogen ions.

9 The negative hydroxide ions pass to the anode. They combine with the **unstable zinc ions,** generating zinc oxide and water.

When all the zinc has converted to oxide and water, the battery is discharged.

Types

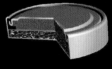

1.5 V

CLOCK

Frequently made of lithium, it is more expensive but takes up less space than alkaline batteries.

1.2 v

RECHARGEABLE

The most used are nickel metal hydride batteries. They have less voltage and a shorter life than alkaline batteries, but they can be recharged many times.

The Turbine

A turbine transforms the energy of fluids passing through it into the rotational motion of an axle. The fluid could be liquid, as in the hydraulic turbines of hydroelectric power plants, or gas, as in steam and gas turbines. The fluid pushes against blades mounted on components called a stator and a rotor. As the fluid pushes against the blades of the rotor, it produces rotational motion that causes the rotor to turn an axle. ●

The operating principle is the same one used in windmills.

How Jet Propulsion Works

➤ The turbine system has four phases: compression of incoming air, combustion, expansion, and exhaust of the gases. The result is thrust.

COLD AIR

FRONT FAN
sucks in great amounts of air, causing compression in the first stage, which eventually becomes thrust.

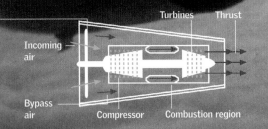

Incoming air

Bypass air

Turbines

Thrust

Compressor

Combustion region

IN PASSENGER AIRPLANES

In large passenger jets, a front fan is added to the compressor. This system is called a turbofan engine.

IN HELICOPTERS, TANKS, AND SHIPS

the impulse of the gases is changed into rotational motion by means of a second turbine.

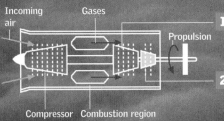

Incoming air

Gases

Propulsion

Compressor

Combustion region

1 Turbine
The force of the gases makes the turbines rotate, thereby turning the compressor.

2 Gear box
Rotates independently and can move a motor, rotor blades (helicopters), or wheels and tracks (tanks).

PROPULSION/DIFFERENT APPLICATIONS

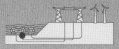

COMMERCIAL AIRPLANES
use a turbofan system to save fuel.

WAR PLANES
use a special type of turbine for greater thrust and speed.

HELICOPTERS
use them to move their rotor blades, which support and propel them.

TANKS
In tanks, like the M1, the turbines turn the wheels that move the treads.

CARS
Formula One cars use exhaust gases to produce additional power.

ENERGY
Turbines are used in dams and rivers to utilize the force of water. They can also harness wind energy or be used in other electric-generation systems.

MATERIAL
They are made with nickel alloys, allowing them to operate at 3,100° F (1,700° C) without deforming.

STARTUP
They are started with pressurized air that is injected from an auxiliary power unit into the compressor. In airplanes, this unit makes the turbine an autonomous source of power.

GASES

PROPULSION

NOZZLE
4.
Exhaust opening for the gases that produce the motion. There are different types of nozzles designed to reduce noise or temperature.

TURBINES
3.
The action of the gas exhaust makes the compressor move and the turbine blades complete one rotation.

COMBUSTION CHAMBER
2.
The hot air is sprayed with fuel, and the fuel ignites because of the elevated temperature inside the chamber. Gases are released at high speed and pressure.

FUEL

COMPRESSED AIR

COMPRESSOR
1.
The blades compress the incoming air, increasing its pressure and temperature and preparing it for combustion.

Energy Resources

Nature is a giant power plant that generates clean, renewable energy. For this reason, faced with rapidly depleting petroleum, natural gas, and coal reserves, experts across the world have developed technologies to utilize alternative energies from the Sun, wind, water, and the interior of the Earth. Norway and Canada already

obtain much of their electricity from hydroelectric power plants. Some architectural designs also seek to take maximum advantage of solar energy to heat homes, offices, and greenhouses.

In some places in the United States and various European countries, wind farms are used to produce electricity. ●

The Earth's Magnetism

The Earth behaves like a giant bar magnet and has a magnetic field with two poles. It is likely that the Earth's magnetism results from the motion of the iron and nickel in its electroconductive core. Another probable origin of the Earth's magnetism lies in the convection currents caused by the heat of the core. The Earth's magnetic field has varied over the course of time. During the last five million years, more than 20 reversals have taken place. The most recent one occurred 700,000 years ago. The interaction of the Earth's magnetic field with the Sun's magnetic field produces phenomena such as the aurora borealis and australis; the interaction can also cause interference in radio-wave transmissions.

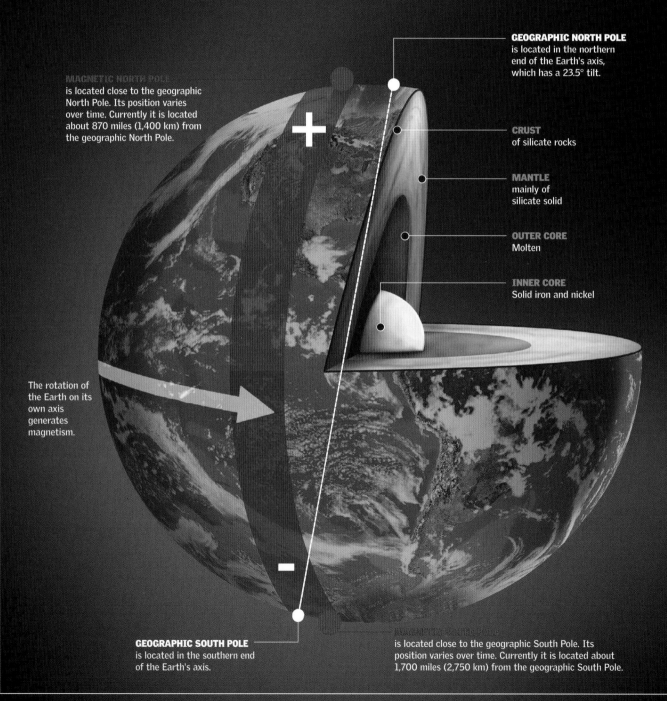

MAGNETIC NORTH POLE
is located close to the geographic North Pole. Its position varies over time. Currently it is located about 870 miles (1,400 km) from the geographic North Pole.

GEOGRAPHIC NORTH POLE
is located in the northern end of the Earth's axis, which has a 23.5° tilt.

CRUST
of silicate rocks

MANTLE
mainly of silicate solid

OUTER CORE
Molten

INNER CORE
Solid iron and nickel

The rotation of the Earth on its own axis generates magnetism.

GEOGRAPHIC SOUTH POLE
is located in the southern end of the Earth's axis.

is located close to the geographic South Pole. Its position varies over time. Currently it is located about 1,700 miles (2,750 km) from the geographic South Pole.

The atmosphere reaches 560 miles (900 km).

MAGNETOSPHERE

The invisible lines of force that form around the Earth. It has an ovoid shape and extends 37,000 miles (60,000 km) from the Earth. Among other things, it protects the Earth from harmful particles radiated by the Sun.

Solar wind with charged atomic particles

The deformation of the magnetosphere is caused by the action of electrically charged particles streaming from the Sun.

The Van Allen belts are bands of ionized atomic particles.

PLANETARY AND SOLAR MAGNETISM

The planets in the solar system have various magnetic fields with varying characteristics.

The four giant planets possess stronger magnetic fields than the Earth.

NEPTUNE	URANUS	SATURN	JUPITER	MARS	EARTH	VENUS	MERCURY	SUN

MARS: It is believed that in the past its magnetic field was stronger.

VENUS: It is the only planet in the solar system that does not have a magnetic field.

MERCURY: It has a weak magnetic field.

SUN: The gases that flow from the Sun's corona produce a magnetic field around it.

SUPERCONDUCTOR MAGNETS

generate magnetic fields, as the Earth does. They are stronger than ordinary electromagnets and can generate more energy. They have many uses, from railway transportation to nuclear medicine.

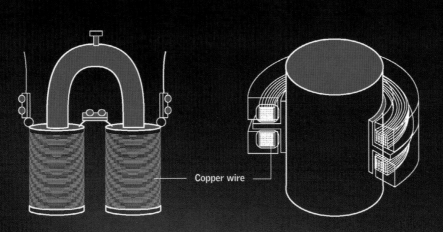

ELECTROMAGNET
Heating of the coil by the wire's electrical resistance results in the loss of energy in the form of heat and wear and tear on the magnet.

Copper wire

SUPERCONDUCTOR
Particle accelerators make use of superconductor magnets and their lack of electric resistance to produce strong magnetic fields.

Ultraviolet Radiation

nvisible to the human eye (but not to many birds, reptiles, and insects), the short wavelengths of this electromagnetic radiation are harmful to living beings. Fortunately the ozone layer in the atmosphere filters out almost all the dangerous radiation but lets through beneficial rays. UV rays are used in astronomy, mineralogy, plague control, spectrophotometry, and the sterilization of surgical material. ●

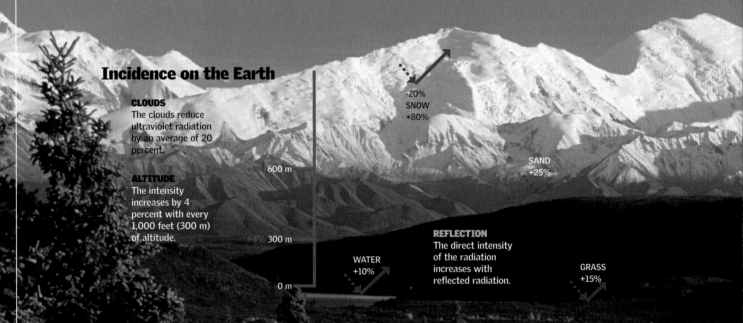

Incidence on the Earth

CLOUDS
The clouds reduce ultraviolet radiation by an average of 20 percent.

ALTITUDE
The intensity increases by 4 percent with every 1,000 feet (300 m) of altitude.

-20%
SNOW
+80%

SAND
+25%

600 m

300 m

0 m

WATER
+10%

REFLECTION
The direct intensity of the radiation increases with reflected radiation.

GRASS
+15%

Effects on Humans

THE SKIN
UV rays can cause sunburn, an inflammation of the skin. Melanin, a dark pigment, helps protect the skin from UV rays. Over time, prolonged exposure to the UV rays in sunlight harms skin fibers and can lead to wrinkling, dryness, and skin cancer.

IMMUNE SYSTEM
Its weakening increases the likelihood of contracting infectious diseases.

EYES
Cataracts and other eyesight disorders

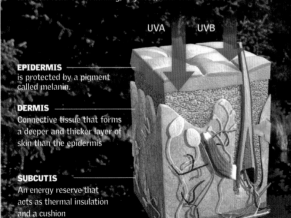

UVA   UVB

EPIDERMIS
is protected by a pigment called melanin.

DERMIS
Connective tissue that forms a deeper and thicker layer of skin than the epidermis

SUBCUTIS
An energy reserve that acts as thermal insulation and a cushion

Animals
Like humans, animals can suffer from skin cancer, weakening of the immune system, and eye injury.

Vegetables
Soy and rice plants exposed to UVB rays are smaller and have lower yield.

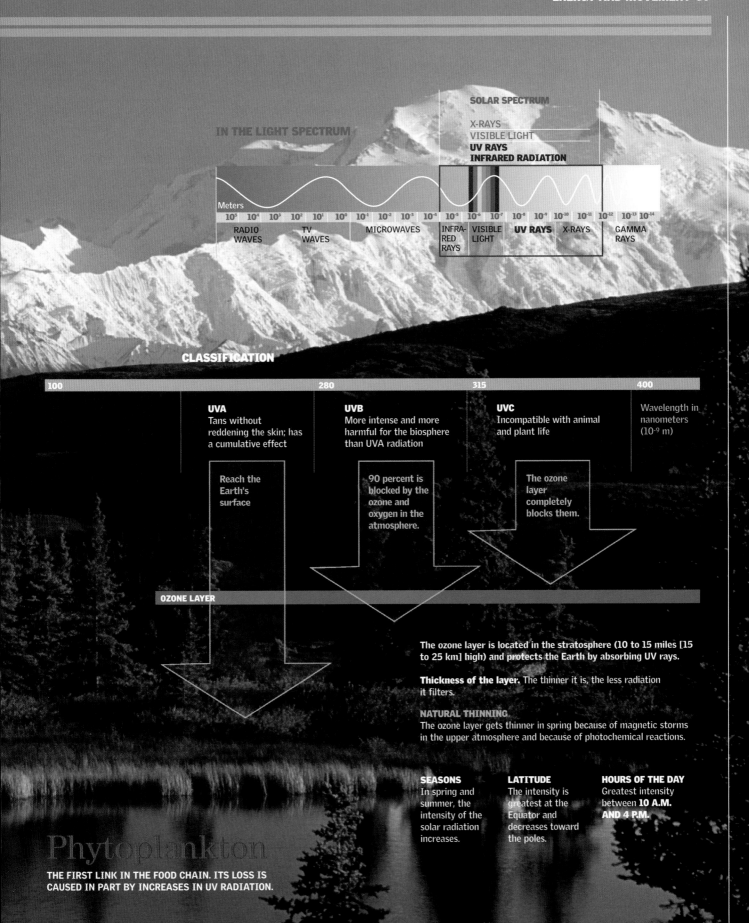

IN THE LIGHT SPECTRUM

SOLAR SPECTRUM
X-RAYS
VISIBLE LIGHT
UV RAYS
INFRARED RADIATION

Meters

| 10^5 | 10^4 | 10^3 | 10^2 | 10^1 | 10^0 | 10^{-1} | 10^{-2} | 10^{-3} | 10^{-4} | 10^{-5} | 10^{-6} | 10^{-7} | 10^{-8} | 10^{-9} | 10^{-10} | 10^{-11} | 10^{-12} | 10^{-13} | 10^{-14} |

RADIO WAVES · TV WAVES · MICROWAVES · INFRA-RED RAYS · VISIBLE LIGHT · UV RAYS · X-RAYS · GAMMA RAYS

CLASSIFICATION

| 100 | 280 | 315 | 400 |

UVA
Tans without reddening the skin; has a cumulative effect

UVB
More intense and more harmful for the biosphere than UVA radiation

UVC
Incompatible with animal and plant life

Wavelength in nanometers (10^{-9} m)

Reach the Earth's surface

90 percent is blocked by the ozone and oxygen in the atmosphere.

The ozone layer completely blocks them.

OZONE LAYER

The ozone layer is located in the stratosphere (10 to 15 miles [15 to 25 km] high) and protects the Earth by absorbing UV rays.

Thickness of the layer. The thinner it is, the less radiation it filters.

NATURAL THINNING
The ozone layer gets thinner in spring because of magnetic storms in the upper atmosphere and because of photochemical reactions.

SEASONS
In spring and summer, the intensity of the solar radiation increases.

LATITUDE
The intensity is greatest at the Equator and decreases toward the poles.

HOURS OF THE DAY
Greatest intensity between **10 A.M. AND 4 P.M.**

Phytoplankton

THE FIRST LINK IN THE FOOD CHAIN. ITS LOSS IS CAUSED IN PART BY INCREASES IN UV RADIATION.

Gravity

his is the name given to the mutual attraction of two objects with mass. It is one of the four fundamental forces observed in nature. The effect of gravity on a body tends to be associated, in common language, with the concept of weight. Gravity is responsible for large-scale movements throughout the universe; it causes, for example, the planets in the solar system to orbit the Sun. In astronautics, the energy of gravitational fields is used to accelerate or slow down space probes, changing their trajectories and allowing them to move toward new, less accessible destinations.

How Gravity Works

 The force that keeps the stars together in the galaxies and our feet firm on the ground

IN SPACE

FIRST LAW
A planet does not move in a straight line, because there is a force (from the Sun) that gravitationally attracts it.

SECOND LAW
The acceleration that this force produces is such that the planet's orbital path is an ellipse that has the Sun as one of its foci.

THIRD LAW
If the Sun exerts a force on the planet, the planet exerts a force on the Sun with the same intensity but in the opposite direction.

Gravity is a property of all bodies with mass (people, things, planets, stars, and so on).

1642-172

ISAAC NEWTON
conceptually unified the dynamics of stars with the Earth's gravitation and untangled the secrets of light and color.

According to legend, a falling apple was Newton's inspiration.

LAW OF UNIVERSAL GRAVITATION
is the attractive gravitational force between two masses in the universe.

DIRECTLY PROPORTIONAL TO THE PRODUCT OF THEIR MASSES

Since the Earth's mass is greater, the force of gravity is more intense.

0.4 s

ON EARTH

How long a ball takes to fall 3 feet (1 m) on the Moon

1.1 s

ON THE MOON

PROPORTIONAL TO THE SQUARE DISTANCE BETWEEN THE MASSES

SPACE

As we move away from the Earth's center, the force of gravity decreases.

In space, the weight of a ball decreases because the force of gravity is less, even though its mass does not change.

EARTH

As speed increases, the friction from air increases until it equals the force of gravity. The terminal velocity of the object has been reached.

AIR RESISTANCE
The force due to the friction of the ball with the air. It increases with the speed of the ball.

Force of gravity

MATHEMATICAL FORMULA

$$F = G \, \frac{Mm}{d^2}$$

Gravity always acts downward toward the Earth's center.

$6.673 \times 10^{-11} \, m^3/(kg \, s^2)$
is the constant of universal gravitation.

Natural Gas

A fter petroleum, natural gas slowly rose to a position of importance in the global balance of energy sources because of its availability and efficiency. It has a reputation of being the cleanest fossil fuel. Technological advances, especially in the discovery of deposits, have produced an explosion in the reserve statistics in the last 15 years. These developments have been accompanied by an ever-increasing dependency on natural gas in different parts of the planet. ●

Phantom Energy

Natural gas is a colorless, odorless fluid that contains between 70 and 90 percent methane, the component that makes it useful as a source of energy.

2 REFINEMENT
The solid and wet components are separated. Then the byproducts, like propane and ethylene, are separated.

1 EXTRACTION
The gas is extracted from the deposit through a hole. When the gas is under pressure, it rises to the surface on its own. When it is not under pressure, it must be pumped.

3 DISTRIBUTION
After being distilled and converted essentially into methane, natural gas is distributed for use through gas pipelines.

4 LIQUEFACTION
When it must be transported by sea or stored, the gas is compressed and cooled to -258° F (-161° C) to liquefy it.

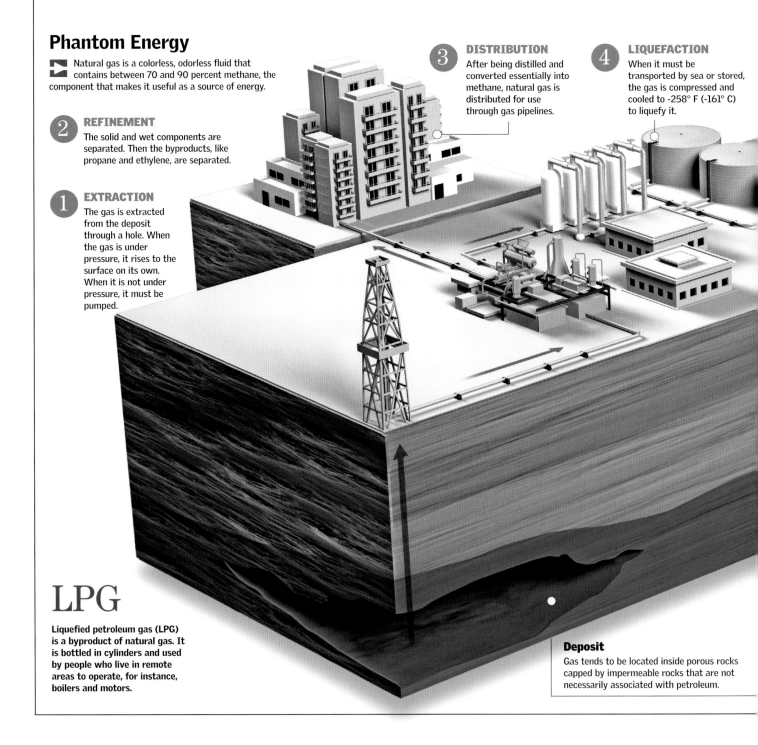

LPG

Liquefied petroleum gas (LPG) is a byproduct of natural gas. It is bottled in cylinders and used by people who live in remote areas to operate, for instance, boilers and motors.

Deposit
Gas tends to be located inside porous rocks capped by impermeable rocks that are not necessarily associated with petroleum.

Lossless Trip

Among the many virtues of natural gas is the efficiency with which it can be transported. From gas deposits, it can be sent thousands of miles by ship or through gas pipelines with minimal losses.

⑦ DISTRIBUTION
The gas reaches residential and commercial consumers.

⑤ TRANSPORT
Large, double-hulled, pressurized ships transport the gas in a liquid state.

1/600
The reduction in volume of natural gas when it is liquefied for storage or transport

⑥ GASIFICATION
After transport, the liquefied gas is returned to the gaseous state to be distributed through a network of gas mains.

Dry gas deposits

Gas chamber

Impermeable rock

Petroleum deposits

Gas chamber

Petroleum

Reserves

The largest reserves of natural gas in the world are found in Russia and the Middle East.

Country	Trillion cubic feet		% of Total
Russia		1,680	27.4
Iran		971	15.9
Qatar		911	14.9
Saudi Arabia		241	3.9
United Arab Emirates		214	3.5
United States		204	3.3
Nigeria		185	3.0
Algeria		161	2.6
Venezuela		151	2.5
Iraq		112	1.8
Indonesia		98	1.6
Norway		84	1.4
Malaysia		75	1.2
Rest of the world		1,037	16.9

6,124
trillion cubic feet is the total of the known reserves in the world.

Petroleum

P etroleum is the main energy source in the developed world. It comes from ancient organic deposits that have been buried in the bowels of the Earth for hundreds of millions of years. Its pure state, called crude oil, is a mix of different hydrocarbons of little use, and hence the oil must first be distilled to separate its components. This valuable resource, which pollutes the atmosphere when burned, is nonrenewable and available only in limited reserves; these characteristics have driven researchers to look for alternative energy sources. ●

Contaminant-gas treatment units

From the Well to the Tank

After its extraction, crude oil is distilled and fractioned into several products, among them gasoline.

Gas flare stack

2 CRUDE OIL STORAGE
The crude oil is stored and then transported to refineries through pipelines or by large tanker ships.

1 EXTRACTION
The oil is pumped from the deposit up to the storage tanks.

3 VAPORIZATION
The crude oil is heated in a boiler up to 752° F (400° C) or more. Once vaporized, it is sent through the distilling tower.

2050
The year the world's oil reserves could run out if the current rate of consumption is maintained and no new discoveries are made.

Storage tanks

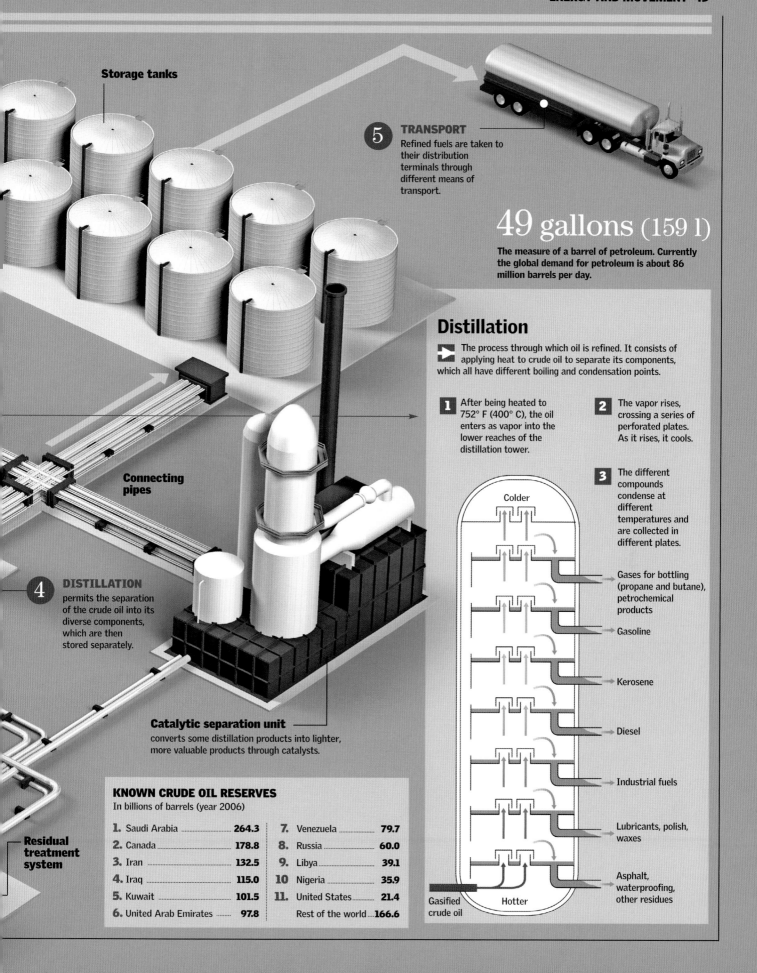

5 **TRANSPORT**
Refined fuels are taken to their distribution terminals through different means of transport.

49 gallons (159 l)

The measure of a barrel of petroleum. Currently the global demand for petroleum is about 86 million barrels per day.

Distillation

The process through which oil is refined. It consists of applying heat to crude oil to separate its components, which all have different boiling and condensation points.

1 After being heated to 752° F (400° C), the oil enters as vapor into the lower reaches of the distillation tower.

2 The vapor rises, crossing a series of perforated plates. As it rises, it cools.

3 The different compounds condense at different temperatures and are collected in different plates.

Colder

Connecting pipes

4 **DISTILLATION**
permits the separation of the crude oil into its diverse components, which are then stored separately.

Catalytic separation unit
converts some distillation products into lighter, more valuable products through catalysts.

Gases for bottling (propane and butane), petrochemical products

Gasoline

Kerosene

Diesel

Industrial fuels

Lubricants, polish, waxes

Asphalt, waterproofing, other residues

Gasified crude oil   Hotter

Residual treatment system

KNOWN CRUDE OIL RESERVES
In billions of barrels (year 2006)

1.	Saudi Arabia	264.3	7.	Venezuela	79.7
2.	Canada	178.8	8.	Russia	60.0
3.	Iran	132.5	9.	Libya	39.1
4.	Iraq	115.0	10	Nigeria	35.9
5.	Kuwait	101.5	11.	United States	21.4
6.	United Arab Emirates	97.8		Rest of the world	166.6

Nuclear Energy

ne of the most efficient and cleanest methods for obtaining electric energy is through a controlled nuclear reaction. Although this technology has been used for half a century, it continues to be at the center of debate because of the risks it poses to the environment and health and because of the highly toxic waste it creates.

Fission

→ The nuclei of certain atoms, like uranium-235, can be broken apart when bombarded by neutrons. In doing so, they release great amounts of energy and new neutrons that can break down the nuclei of other atoms, generating a chain reaction.

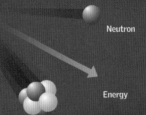

Neutron

Neutron

Neutron

Energy

Moderator
To achieve the breakdown of the nucleus, the neutrons must collide with it at a specific speed, which is governed by a moderating substance, such as water, heavy water, graphite, and so on.

Nucleus of a uranium-235 atom

Generation of Energy

→ The purpose of nuclear fission is to create very hot steam to operate turbines and electrical generators. The high temperatures are achieved by using nuclear energy from the reactor.

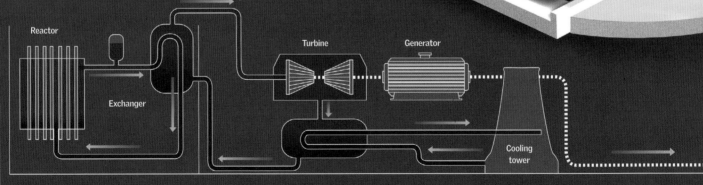

Reactor

Exchanger

Turbine

Generator

Cooling tower

1 **Water**
Pressurized water, together with the moderator, is pumped through the core of the reactor, and the temperature of the core increases by hundreds of degrees.

2 **Steam**
The resulting steam enters an exchanger, where it heats water until it too is converted into steam.

3 **Electricity**
The steam enters the turbines and makes them run. The turbines drive the generator that produces electricity.

4 **Recycling**
The steam condenses into liquid water and is reused.

Mobile crane
moves the mechanism that replenishes the reactor with nuclear fuel.

Reactor core
contains the radioactive fuel and is where the nuclear reaction takes place.

370,000

Power, in megawatts (MW), generated by nuclear energy throughout the world

Uranium

➤ In nature, uranium appears associated with other minerals. In addition, only 0.7 percent of uranium is the isotope uranium-235, necessary for nuclear fission. The proportion of uranium-235 must be increased 3 to 5 percent in a process called enrichment.

1 The original mineral is treated until a substance called yellowcake is obtained that is 80 percent uranium.

2 During conversion, first uranium tetrafluoride (UF4) and then uranium hexafluoride (UF6) are obtained.

3 The gaseous uranium hexafluoride is spun repeatedly in a centrifuge until it attains the desired concentration of uranium-235.

4 The enriched uranium gas is solidified again.

5 Through compaction, pellets of enriched uranium are obtained that can be used as fuel in nuclear reactors.

6 The pellets are put into hollow bars that are later placed in the core of the nuclear reactor.

UF4

UF4

Separators
separate the liquid water from the steam.

Steam to the turbines

Hot water pipes

Cold water pipes

Pump
maintains the circulation of the fluids in the system.

Transformer

5 **Transport**
Before transmitting electricity, a transformer increases its voltage.

436

The number of nuclear plants operating throughout the world. More than 30 are in various stages of construction.

Fuel rod

Uranium pellets

Biofuels

G asoline or diesel with added alcohol (ethanol) produced from crops such as corn appear more and more promising as solutions to the problems posed by the eventual exhaustion of the Earth's petroleum reserves, as well as the high cost of fossil fuels on the global market. However, this type of energy presents new challenges. One item of environmental concern is the possibility that massive exploitation of biofuels could lead to the replacement of jungles and woodlands with single-crop plantations meant only for the production of raw plant materials. ●

Ethanol

This is the alcohol in the medicine cabinets of our homes. It can be used in its pure form as a fuel or combined with gasoline in different proportions. The greater its purity, the greater are the engine modifications required to burn the fuel. Two common mixtures are E10 and E85, which have 10 percent and 85 percent ethanol, respectively.

2 MILLING
The raw material is milled, and the resulting flour is mixed with water. Later an enzyme is added that helps convert starch into sugar.

3 COOKING
The mixture is cooked at 300° F (150° C) (sterilization) and is finally cooled with a water-refrigeration system.

4 FERMENTATION
Yeast is added to convert sugar into ethanol. This process, which produces heat and carbon dioxide, lasts 60 hours. When finished, the mixture, called mash, is 15 percent ethanol.

1 HARVEST
Sugarcane, beets, corn, yucca, potatoes, and even wood can be used, with varying degrees of efficiency, to produce ethanol.

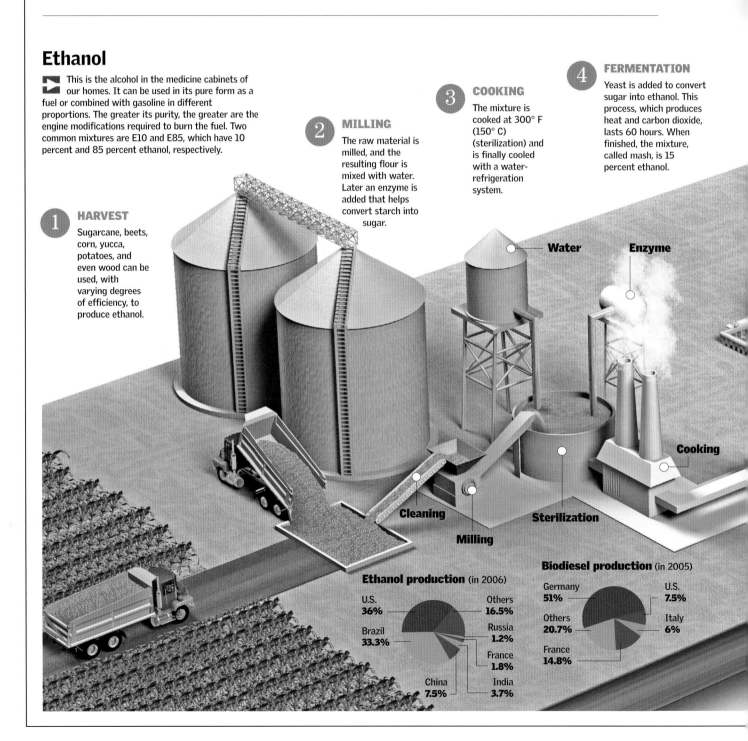

Water

Enzyme

Cooking

Cleaning

Milling

Sterilization

Ethanol production (in 2006)
U.S. 36%
Brazil 33.3%
China 7.5%
Others 16.5%
Russia 1.2%
France 1.8%
India 3.7%

Biodiesel production (in 2005)
Germany 51%
Others 20.7%
France 14.8%
U.S. 7.5%
Italy 6%

KERNEL OF CORN

HULL
protects the seed from water, insects, and microorganisms.

ENDOSPERM
represents 70 percent of the weight of the dry grain. It contains starch, the substance used to produce ethanol.

GERM
The most valuable and the only living part of the grain. In addition to containing the genetic material, vitamins, and minerals, it is 25 percent oil.

5 DISTILLATION
The mixture is distilled first by evaporation to obtain 96 percent pure ethanol. It is later distilled by a molecular filtration process that can produce ethanol that is almost entirely pure. A 5 percent gasoline mixture is used for transportation.

Byproducts

are generated during the production of ethanol. Anhydrous carbon is used in the manufacture of soft drinks. The stillage, a very nutritious residue, is used to feed cattle.

55 pounds (25 kg) of corn + 4 gallons (15 l) of water

PRODUCE

2.8 gallons (10.5 l) of ethanol + 18.5 pounds (8.4 kg) of carbon dioxide + 18.5 pounds (8.4 kg) of stillage

6 USE
Ethanol is added to gasolines in different proportions to be used in vehicles. Gasolines with ethanol content between 10 and 30 percent do not require vehicle engines to have special modifications.

Yeast

Carbon dioxide collection

Fermentation tanks

Gasoline

Distillation

Refrigeration

70%
of the world's ethanol production is accounted for by Brazil and the United States. In Brazil, ethanol is made from sugarcane, and in the United States, it is made from corn.

Solar Energy

The harnessing of solar energy to produce electricity and heat for everyday use is gaining popularity. Applications of this clean, unlimited form of energy range from charging batteries in telecommunications satellites, to public transportation, all the way to the solar households being built in greater numbers throughout the world.

ENERGY REGULATOR

Photovoltaic Energy

The energy obtained from sunlight. Requires the use of solar or photovoltaic cells.

SOLAR CELL

It is essentially formed by a thin layer of semiconductor material (silicon, for example), where the photovoltaic effect—the transformation of light into electrical energy—takes place.

1 The Sun shines on the cell. Some very energetic photons move the electrons and make them jump to the illuminated face of the cell.

2 The negatively charged electrons generate a negative terminal on the illuminated face and leave an empty space in the positively charged dark face (positive terminal).

3 Once the circuit is closed, there is a constant flow of electrons (electric current) from the negative terminal to the positive one.

4 The current is maintained as long as the Sun illuminates the cell.

- Photon
- Electron (-)

Electricity to the network

Upper metallic grid contact (negative electrode)

Upper metallic grid contact (positive electrode)

Negative contact (-)

Negative semiconductor (-) (mostly silicon)

Active charge carrier zone

Positive semiconductor (+) (mostly silicon)

Positive contact (+)

Investment

One of the main problems with using solar energy on an industrial scale is the high startup cost required to harness the energy; this cost keeps solar energy from competing with other cheaper energy sources.

Solar Heating

Another use of sunlight is as a source for heating water as well as for heating homes. In this case, solar collectors are used; unlike photovoltaic cells, the solar collectors do not produce electric energy.

180° F (82° C)

The maximum temperature a solar collector can reach when used to heat a house or to simply boil water

THE COLLECTOR

works using the greenhouse effect. It absorbs the heat from the Sun and then prevents this heat from being lost. In doing so, it warms a pipe, through which the fluid (water or gas) flows, that in turn heats a tank (exchanger).

Protective Cover

is formed by one or several glass plates. It lets sunlight through but retains the heat accumulated in the collector.

Absorption Plate

contains tubing, generally made of copper, through which the fluid heated in the collector flows.

Thermal Plate

The reflecting material and the black color absorb as much of the Sun's heat as possible. The protective plate then prevents any loss.

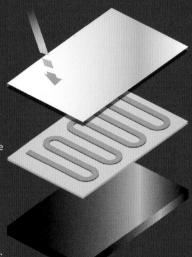

HOT WATER AND HEATING CIRCUIT

1 The hot liquid flows from the collector through a circuit.

2 It enters a heat exchanger, where it heats the water used in the house.

3 The water leaves the exchanger at a temperature suitable for domestic use or for heating a house.

4 A pump takes the cooled fluid to the collector, where it repeats the cycle.

Hot-water output

Cold-water intake

Other Applications

In almost every system powered by electricity, solar energy can play a central role without endangering the environment. Although this technology is presently more expensive to use than coal, natural gas, or petroleum, this difference in cost could change soon.

Space

Its use has extended to probes and satellites so that today hardly any spacecraft are designed without solar panels.

Transportation

The great challenge. Many prototypes of solar cars have been built, and some cities are already experimenting with buses.

Electronics

Calculators, watches, radios, flashlights, and so on. Almost any battery-powered device can be powered by solar energy.

Wind Energy

One of the most promising renewable energy resources is the use of wind to produce electricity by driving enormous wind turbines (windmills). Eolic power is an inexhaustible, clean, nonpolluting source of energy with more advantages than disadvantages. The most important disadvantages are our inability to predict precisely the force and direction of winds and the possibly negative impact that groups of large towers could have on the local landscape. ●

The Turbine

converts the wind into electrical energy through the use of simple technology based on mechanical gears.

1 The wind
moves the blades of the wind turbine, producing mechanical energy, which is then converted into electrical energy.

Brakes
are activated when the winds surpass 74 miles per hour (120 km/h), preventing damage to the wind turbine.

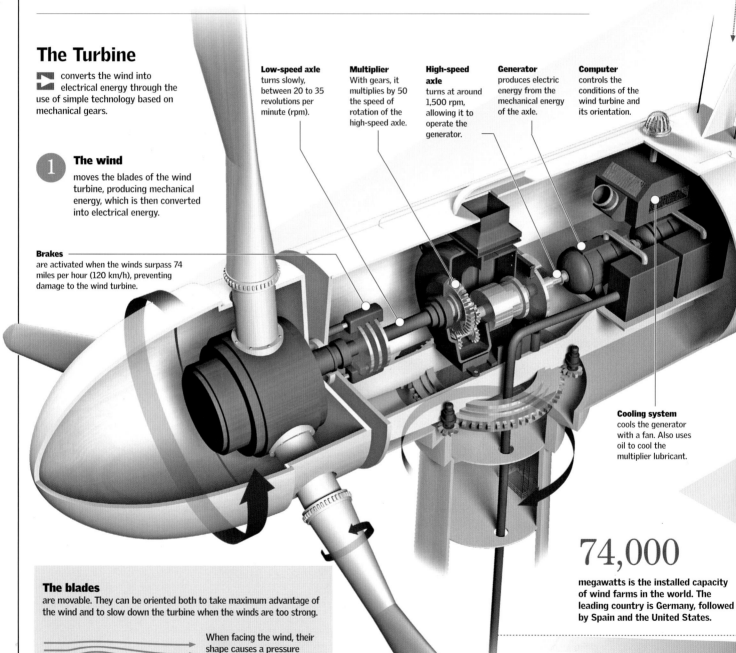

Low-speed axle
turns slowly, between 20 to 35 revolutions per minute (rpm).

Multiplier
With gears, it multiplies by 50 the speed of rotation of the high-speed axle.

High-speed axle
turns at around 1,500 rpm, allowing it to operate the generator.

Generator
produces electric energy from the mechanical energy of the axle.

Computer
controls the conditions of the wind turbine and its orientation.

Cooling system
cools the generator with a fan. Also uses oil to cool the multiplier lubricant.

74,000

megawatts is the installed capacity of wind farms in the world. The leading country is Germany, followed by Spain and the United States.

The blades
are movable. They can be oriented both to take maximum advantage of the wind and to slow down the turbine when the winds are too strong.

When facing the wind, their shape causes a pressure difference between the two faces of the wind turbine's blades. The pressure on the blades produces a force that turns the rotor.

2 Energy
The electric energy produced by the generator goes down the cables to a converter.

Wind Turbines

These modern, large wind turbines, between 150 and 200 feet (45 and 60 m) high, tend to be grouped in windy, isolated, mostly deserted regions. The most modern wind turbines can generate 500 to 2,000 kW of power.

High terrain, free of obstacles, is ideal for wind turbines, because the wind blows freely there and reaches the wind turbines without turbulence.

Blades
measure, on average, 130 feet (40 m) in length. Three-blade rotors have proven to be the most efficient design.

The wind turbines are grouped into wind farms to maximize the potential of transmitting energy from only one location. This has the advantage of lowering costs and reducing environmental impact on the landscape.

The Journey of Electricity

The energy produced in wind farms can travel through the main power grid together with energy generated by other sources.

Wind turbines

The transformer increases by several thousand volts the voltage from the turbines.

The collection plant receives the energy from all the transformers.

Nearby cities receive the energy directly from the collection plant.

Substations receive the energy from the collection plant and increase the voltage by hundreds of thousands of times for transmission to distant cities.

3 **Grid**
After leaving the wind farm, the electric energy can be incorporated into the main distribution grid.

4 **Homes**
The electricity reaches the residential distribution grid and finally homes.

Hydroelectric Energy

About 20 percent of the world's electricity is generated by the force of rivers through the use of hydroelectric power plants. This technology, used since the 19th century, employs a renewable, nonpolluting resource, although the technology's impact on the environment is high. According to the United Nations, two thirds of the world's hydroelectric potential is being used, especially in North America and Europe.

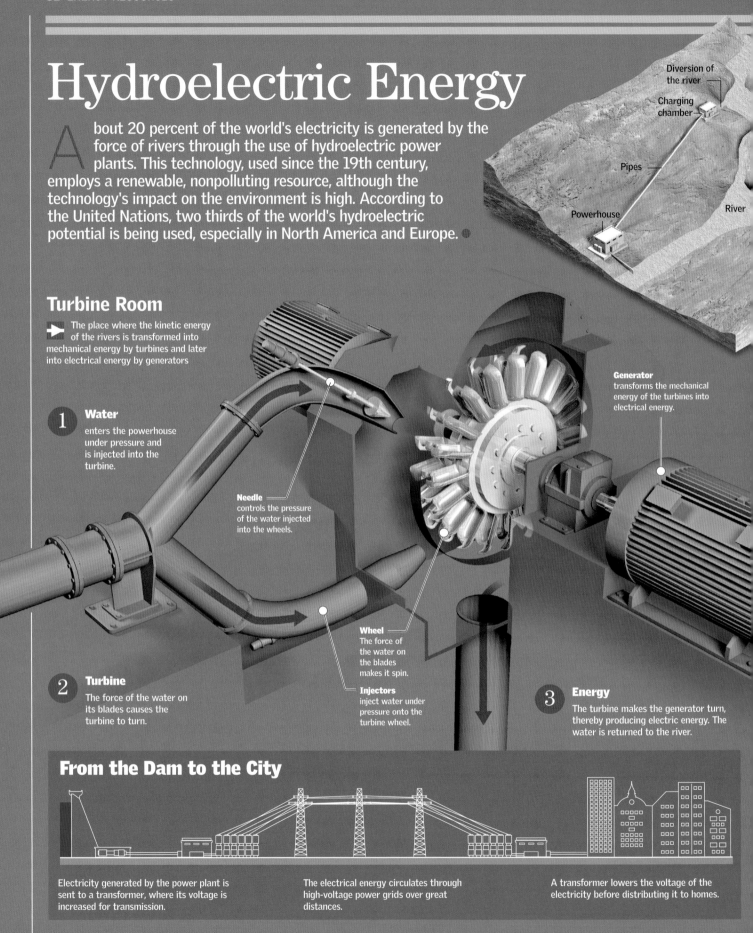

Diversion of the river

Charging chamber

Pipes

River

Powerhouse

Turbine Room

The place where the kinetic energy of the rivers is transformed into mechanical energy by turbines and later into electrical energy by generators

1 Water
enters the powerhouse under pressure and is injected into the turbine.

Needle
controls the pressure of the water injected into the wheels.

Generator
transforms the mechanical energy of the turbines into electrical energy.

Wheel
The force of the water on the blades makes it spin.

Injectors
inject water under pressure onto the turbine wheel.

2 Turbine
The force of the water on its blades causes the turbine to turn.

3 Energy
The turbine makes the generator turn, thereby producing electric energy. The water is returned to the river.

From the Dam to the City

Electricity generated by the power plant is sent to a transformer, where its voltage is increased for transmission.

The electrical energy circulates through high-voltage power grids over great distances.

A transformer lowers the voltage of the electricity before distributing it to homes.

Bypass Plant

1 Does not have a reservoir. It simply takes advantage of the available flow of water and thus is at the mercy of seasonal variations in water flow. It also cannot take advantage of occasional surplus water.

Reservoir

Pipes
Dam
Powerhouse

Plants with Reservoirs

2 The presence of a reservoir, formed by a containment dam, guarantees a constant flow of water—and, therefore, of energy—independent of variations in water level.

1 The water enters the powerhouse and turns the turbines. The generators produce electricity.

2 Once used, the water is returned to the river.

Powerhouse
Reservoir
Output duct
Pipes
Generator Turbine

China

The world's largest producer of hydroelectricity (95,000 MW installed), followed by the United States, Canada, and Brazil

Pumping Plant

3 has two reservoirs located at different levels. In this way, the water can be reused, which allows a more efficient management of water resources.

1 The water goes from the upper reservoir to the lower one, generating electricity in the process.

Powerhouse
Reservoir
Second reservoir
Pipes
Turbine

2 In off-peak hours, the water is pumped to the first reservoir to be reused.

Powerhouse
Reservoir
Second reservoir
Pipes
Turbine

Reservoir
Dam
Pipes
Powerhouse
Second reservoir

22,500

The planned hydroelectric capacity in megawatts of China's Three Gorges Dam, scheduled for completion in 2009. The previous record holder was the 12,600-MW Itaipú Dam on the border between Paraguay and Brazil.

Geothermal Energy

s one of the cleanest and most promising sources of energy. The first geothermal plant started operating more than 100 years ago. Geothermal plants generate electricity from the heat that emanates from the Earth's interior. Geothermal power plants, however, suffer from some limitations, such as the fact that they must be constructed in regions with high volcanic activity. The possibility of this kind of plant becoming defunct due to a reduction in such volcanic activity is always present. ●

Types of Geothermal Deposits

Geothermal deposits are classified by their temperature and by the resource they provide (water or steam).

°F
700
560
600
550
500
450
400
350
300
250
200
176
100
32
0

Dry-Steam Deposits
They are the most efficient, although the least common. They produce steam at high temperature and pressure.

High-Temperature Deposits
The greater the temperature of the water in the deposit, the greater the efficiency of the plant in producing electric energy. Those of medium-high temperatures require binary-cycle power plants.

Low-Temperature Deposits
With temperatures lower than 176° F (80° C), they are useful for meeting domestic needs, such as heating or producing agricultural commodities.

Types of Power Plants

Not all geothermal power plants are the same. Their characteristics depend on the type of geothermal deposit from where the resource is extracted.

DRY-STEAM POWER PLANT
Some deposits provide water directly instead of steam. The water is at very high temperatures and is used to generate electricity. Power plants of this type save a step by not having to convert water into steam.

Axle to generator

2 Generation
Upon entering the powerhouse, the steam moves a turbine, which then moves an electrical generator.

3 Transport
The electricity obtained is transmitted through high-voltage power lines after going through a transformer.

4 Recycling
The used steam is condensed (converted into water) and reinjected into the deposit.

Deposits
Accumulation of underground water and steam, sometimes contained in cracks or porous rocks, are heated by the magma and can be used as energy resources.

1 Steam
The steam rises from the deposit under its own pressure.

Cooling room

Condensers

Turbine room

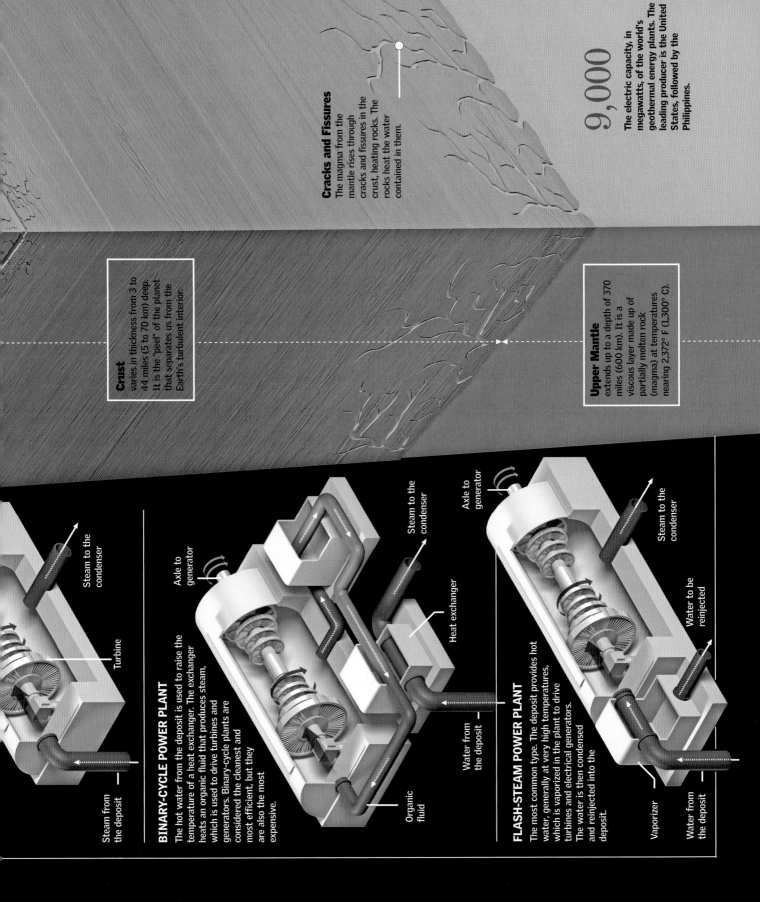

Cracks and Fissures
The magma from the mantle rises through cracks and fissures in the crust, heating rocks. The rocks heat the water contained in them.

Crust
varies in thickness from 3 to 44 miles (5 to 70 km) deep. It is the "peel" of the planet that separates us from the Earth's turbulent interior.

Upper Mantle
extends up to a depth of 370 miles (600 km). It is a viscous layer made up of partially molten rock (magma) at temperatures nearing 2,372° F (1,300° C).

9,000

The electric capacity, in megawatts, of the world's geothermal energy plants. The leading producer is the United States, followed by the Philippines.

BINARY-CYCLE POWER PLANT

The hot water from the deposit is used to raise the temperature of a heat exchanger. The exchanger heats an organic fluid that produces steam, which is used to drive turbines and generators. Binary-cycle plants are considered the cleanest and most efficient, but they are also the most expensive.

Steam to the condenser

Axle to generator

Heat exchanger

Steam from the deposit

Turbine

Water from the deposit

Organic fluid

FLASH-STEAM POWER PLANT

The most common type. The deposit provides hot water, generally at very high temperatures, which is vaporized in the plant to drive turbines and electrical generators. The water is then condensed and reinjected into the deposit.

Axle to generator

Steam to the condenser

Water to be reinjected

Vaporizer

Water from the deposit

56 ENERGY RESOURCES

Tidal Energy

The variations in the tides and the force of the oceans' waves signify an enormous energy potential for generating electricity without emitting polluting gases into the atmosphere or depleting resources, as happens in the case of fossil fuels. Tidal plants are similar to hydroelectric plants. They have a water-retention dam (which crosses an estuary from shore to shore) and a powerhouse where the turbines and generators to produce electricity are located. ●

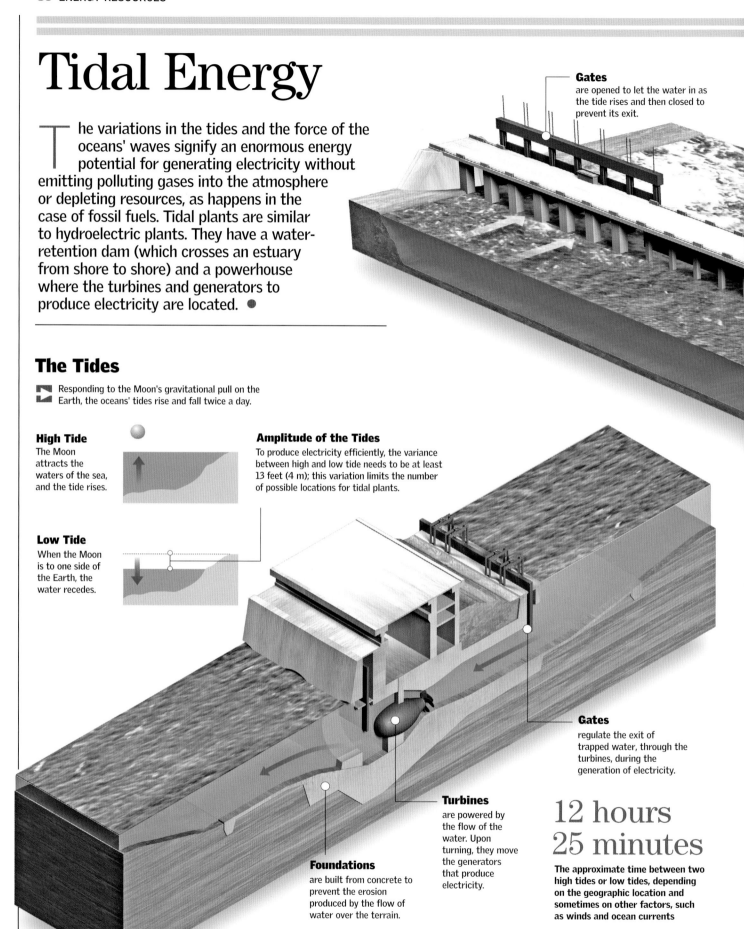

Gates
are opened to let the water in as the tide rises and then closed to prevent its exit.

The Tides

Responding to the Moon's gravitational pull on the Earth, the oceans' tides rise and fall twice a day.

High Tide
The Moon attracts the waters of the sea, and the tide rises.

Low Tide
When the Moon is to one side of the Earth, the water recedes.

Amplitude of the Tides
To produce electricity efficiently, the variance between high and low tide needs to be at least 13 feet (4 m); this variation limits the number of possible locations for tidal plants.

Gates
regulate the exit of trapped water, through the turbines, during the generation of electricity.

Turbines
are powered by the flow of the water. Upon turning, they move the generators that produce electricity.

Foundations
are built from concrete to prevent the erosion produced by the flow of water over the terrain.

12 hours 25 minutes

The approximate time between two high tides or low tides, depending on the geographic location and sometimes on other factors, such as winds and ocean currents

Tidal Power Plant
The turbines, which power the generators, are found inside the plant. They convert the kinetic energy of the water into mechanical energy and then into electrical energy.

Dam
crosses the estuary or bay from shore to shore. It retains the water during high tide.

Location of the Dam

The power plant needs be located in a river outlet to the sea (estuary) or in a narrow bay—places that have above-average tidal amplitude (the variance between low tide and high tide).

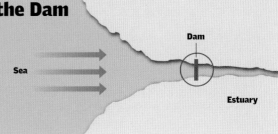

Sea

Dam

Estuary

Electrical Substation
increases the voltage of the generated power before its transmission.

High-Voltage Grid
takes the electrical energy to the regions where it will be consumed.

Rance
The largest tidal power plant in the world. It was built in northern France in 1967 and has an electrical generating capacity of 240 megawatts.

Generation of Electricity

As in a hydroelectric power plant, the trapped water turns a turbine that operates the generators.

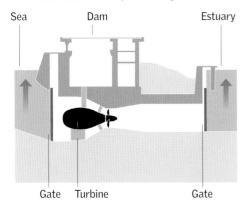

Sea — Dam — Estuary

Gate   Turbine   Gate

 High Tide
During high tide, the level of the water rises in the estuary. The gates of the dam are opened to let the water in.

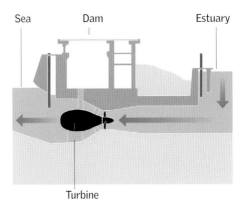

Sea — Dam — Estuary

Gate   Turbine   Gate

 Water Reservoir
Once high tide is complete, the water level in the estuary begins to drop. The gates of the dam are closed to prevent the trapped water from escaping.

Sea — Dam — Estuary

Turbine

3 **Generation**
During low tide, the trapped water is released and it passes through the system of turbines that power the electrical generators.

Biodigesters

When anaerobic bacteria (bacteria that do not require oxygen to live) decompose organic material through processes such as rotting and fermentation, they release biogas that can be used as an energy resource for heating and for generating electricity. They also create mud with very high nutritional value, which can be used in agriculture or fish production. This technology appears promising as an energy alternative for rural and isolated regions, where, in addition to serving the energy needs of the populace, it helps recycle organic wastes.

The Reactor

 is a closed chamber where the bacteria break down the waste. The generated gas (called biogas) and the fertilizing mud are collected for later use.

2 Digestion chamber
Where the bacteria ferment the waste. They produce gas and fertilizing mud.

3 Biogas
is a product of the process that contains methane and carbon dioxide. It is used for cooking, heating, and generating electricity.

4 Fertilizing mud
Very rich in nutrients and odorless, it is ideal for agricultural uses.

1 Waste
The organic wastes are introduced into the reactor and mixed with water.

Dome
is built underground and can be lined with concrete, brick, or stone.

Biogas

Pathogens

Laboratory tests demonstrated that the biodigestion process kills up to 85 percent of the harmful pathogenic agents present in the organic waste, pathogens which would otherwise be released into the environment.

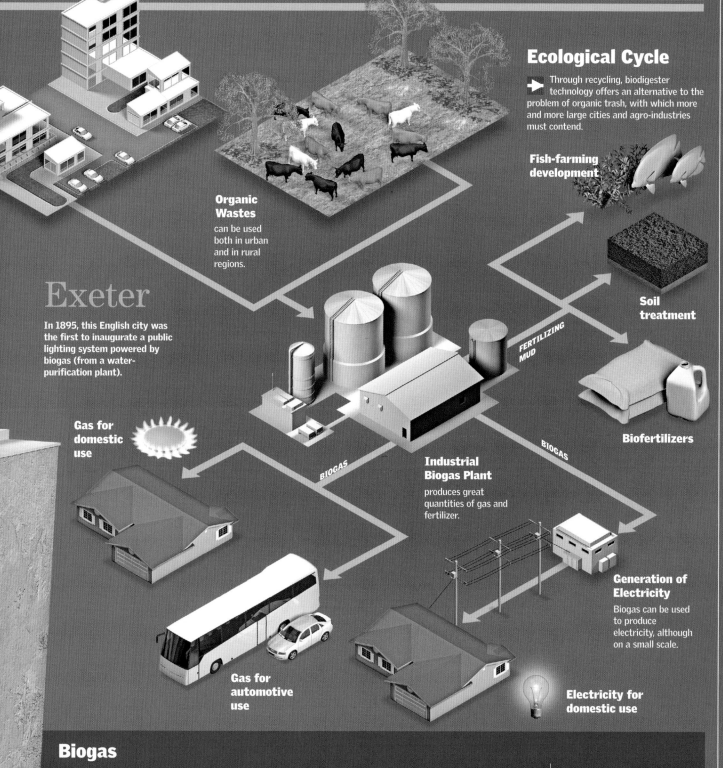

Ecological Cycle

Through recycling, biodigester technology offers an alternative to the problem of organic trash, with which more and more large cities and agro-industries must contend.

Fish-farming development

Soil treatment

Biofertilizers

Organic Wastes can be used both in urban and in rural regions.

Exeter

In 1895, this English city was the first to inaugurate a public lighting system powered by biogas (from a water-purification plant).

Gas for domestic use

FERTILIZING MUD

BIOGAS

Industrial Biogas Plant produces great quantities of gas and fertilizer.

Generation of Electricity

Biogas can be used to produce electricity, although on a small scale.

Gas for automotive use

Electricity for domestic use

Biogas

The gaseous product of biodigestion, it is made up of a mixture of gases whose makeup depends on the composition of the wastes and the break-down process.

55-70%
Methane (CH_4)
The energy-producing component of biogas

30-45%
Carbon Dioxide (CO_2)
A greenhouse gas. It must be removed from biogas for certain uses.

1-10%
Hydrogen (H_2)
Gas present in the atmosphere

0.5-3%
Nitrogen (N_2)
Gas present in the atmosphere

0.1%
Sulfuric Acid (H_2S)
Corrosive and highly polluting agent. It has to be removed.

Equivalencies

1 lb biogas + 1 lb biogas + 1 lb biogas = 1 lb gasoline

The energy potential contained in one pound of gasoline can be obtained from three pounds of organic wastes.

Fission and Chain Reaction

This weapon of mass destruction derives its energy from nuclear reactions. It was used for the first time against Japan, marking the end of World War II and the destruction of the cities of Hiroshima and Nagasaki. In addition to the massive loss of human life at the moment of detonation, many cases of cancer and genetic repercussions followed in the adjacent areas affected by radioactivity. Apparently the horror of witnessing what an atomic bomb could do was not enough, as today many countries have atomic arsenals even more powerful than the bombs used in 1945. ●

The Hiroshima Bomb

▶ It exploded on August 6, 1945, at a height of 1,870 feet (570 m) over the downtown of this Japanese city, taking more than 70,000 lives. It was a fission bomb.

Name	Little Boy
Type	Fission
Power	14.5 kilotons
Weight	4.4 tons

10.5 feet
(3.2 m)

2.4 feet
(0.74 m)

1 DETONATION
An altimeter determines the appropriate height for the explosion and detonates a charge of common explosives; this process impels the projectile toward the atomic explosive.

2 REACTION
The projectile travels through the gun tube and impacts the uranium-235 contained inside the generator. This is what initiates the nuclear chain reaction.

3 EXPLOSION
The chain reaction occurs in a fraction of a second, releasing enormous amounts of energy as heat and lethal radiation.

WARHEAD
Made of uranium-235, it is highly fissile.

GUN TUBE

COMPRESSOR
concentrates the chain reaction so that the greatest amount of atomic explosive can undergo fission before the explosion.

ATOMIC EXPLOSIVE
Compact sphere of uranium-235. Its power equals 14,500 tons of TNT (trinitrotoluene).

Fission and Chain Reaction

Nuclear fission divides the nucleus of the uranium atom by bombarding it with neutrons.

1 A neutron strikes the nucleus of a uranium-235 atom.

2 The nucleus splits in two, releasing three neutrons and an enormous amount of energy.

3 The three neutrons that were released collide with other uranium-235 nuclei, which then divide and release more neutrons and energy. The chain reaction is sustained in this way until the uranium is depleted.

The Fusion Bomb

Even more powerful atomic bombs use a different type of nuclear reaction—the fusion of hydrogen. That is why they are also known as hydrogen bombs. They have a power of up to 9,000 kilotons.

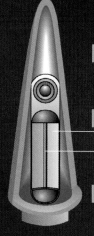

1 DETONATION
A small atomic fission bomb explodes, generating large amounts of heat inside the container.

2 REACTION
The heat compresses the deuterium (hydrogen isotope) against the rod of plutonium, causing fusion.

3 EXPLOSION
The fusion of deuterium takes place in a fraction of a second, causing the explosion.

NUCLEAR ARSENALS

During the Cold War in the second half of the 20th century, the United States and the Soviet Union built large arsenals of nuclear weapons. In addition, several other countries developed nuclear-weapon capabilities. Today it is believed that the United States and Russia (which maintained control of the former Soviet Union's weapons) each have more than 5,000 deployed nuclear warheads with perhaps as many in storage. France, Britain, and China are each estimated to have more than 100 nuclear weapons. India and Pakistan have publicly tested nuclear weapons and may have more than a dozen each.

DAMAGE SCALE

Comparison between two nuclear explosions of differing power

7 MILES (12 KM)	4.6 MILES (7.5 KM)	2.7 MILES (4.3 KM)	1.7 MILES (2.7 KM)

FUSION BOMB
1,000 KILOTONS

0.5 MILE (0.8 KM)
1.3 MILES (2.1 KM)
2.4 MILES (3.9 KM)
3.2 MILES (5.1 KM)

HIROSHIMA
14.5 KILOTONS

■ TOTAL VAPORIZATION
■ TOTAL DESTRUCTION
■ SEVERE DAMAGE
□ SEVERE FIRES

THE ATOMIC MUSHROOM CLOUD

is formed by the shock wave, which absorbs the dust of everything that was burned.

46,000 feet (14,000 m)

29,029 feet (8,848 m)

Mushroom cloud of Hiroshima

Mount Everest

Uses and Applications

Human beings are nomadic by nature, thus their desire to explore made them develop efficient means of transportation that covered great distances very early in their history. However, it has been only in the past few centuries, as inventors began to make use of new scientific knowledge, that such machines have flourished. These

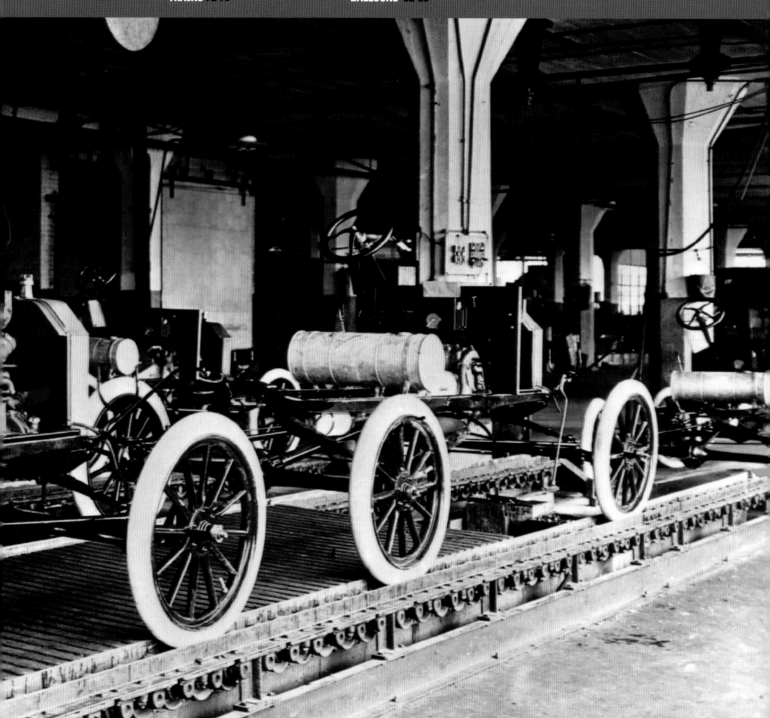

new means of transportation made further discoveries possible, which in turn gave rise to even newer means of transportation, and so on. From sailing ships, which move with the wind, to ocean liners, from extremely efficient bicycles to powerful trains, we present to you the types of transportation that have made history. ●

Doppler Radar

The radar's effective range and use of the Doppler effect—a physical phenomenon postulated in 1842—create an efficient system able to detect moving objects from afar. Doppler radars can determine the speed and direction of a target, making these machines ideal for both civil and military purposes. The introduction of Doppler radars revolutionized meteorology, allowing humans to follow every development of storm patterns for the first time in history and helping people respond quickly and safely to many kinds of natural disasters. ●

The Doppler Effect

Whenever any kind of electromagnetic-wave generator/receiver is turned on, it vibrates, and the waves it emits differ in wavelength from those it receives. This phenomenon is known as the Doppler effect.

Pitch of a car engine

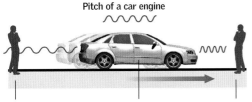

Person 1
As the source of the wave moves away from the listener, the wavelength increases with respect to the listener, and the pitch decreases.

Conductor
always hears the same pitch, because it comes from a constant distance.

Person 2
As the source of the wave approaches the listener, the wave's pitch increases.

The waves emitted by the radar change wavelength when they collide with moving raindrops.

AIRPLANES
are equipped with Doppler radars that inform pilots about areas of heaviest precipitation in storm clouds so that the pilot can choose the safest route to the aircraft's destination.

How Doppler Radar Works

Doppler radar interprets changes in the wavelength of the radio waves it emits. These changes in wavelength are caused when the waves sent from the radar are reflected by a moving object.

Emission
The radar emits radio waves of a known wavelength. If the waves encounter an object, they are reflected.

Reception
The waves reflected from a moving object change wavelength, which the radar correctly interprets as movement.

Bats

have a type of biological Doppler radar. They emit sound waves, which bounce off possible prey, allowing the bats to determine an obstruction's speed and direction.

Reach

Depending on its type, a radar's range can vary from tens to thousands of miles.

Direction of the storm

Following the Storm

Today Doppler radars are used to discover the speed and other characteristics of storms.

1 Detection
A Doppler weather radar beams electromagnetic waves into the storm. The waves' responses to various forms of water, such as raindrops and ice, reveal the density and composition of clouds and can, for example, detect the presence of hail.

2 Measurements
The Doppler effect allows meteorologists to determine a storm's velocity, or speed, and direction, as well as the velocities of internal wind currents.

3 Analysis
A second Doppler radar station obtains data from a different direction, allowing more precise analysis of the data. Then all the data from the different stations are combined and converted into numbers and graphs for a more accurate reading.

Other Applications

Doppler radars are used in anticollision systems of ships and airplanes and as portable traffic-control radars. Doppler radars are also used in medical, military, and underwater research, among other applications.

Traffic
Police use portable Doppler radars to monitor the speed of passing vehicles. Doppler radars are handy tools for verifying the speed of automobiles from any location.

Navigation
Ships and airplanes use Doppler radar systems to scan nearby traffic for possible collision risks. The radars work in tandem with automatic emergency exit systems.

Medicine
Doppler systems have been introduced in diagnostic ultrasound scanning. They can provide visual feedback of movements within the body, as in the circulatory system—even in the heart and brain.

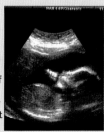

Crash Test Dummies

To assess the risks that automobile passengers could experience in collisions, mannequins—designed to resemble human beings of different sizes and weights—are used. They are fitted with aluminum bones and muscles, as well as with rubber skin. These dummies are equipped with sensors that collect data of every aspect of the collision (acceleration and deceleration effects, among other things). In this way, biomechanical engineers can evaluate possible injuries that real occupants of a vehicle could sustain in similar collisions. These robotic mannequins, which have helped to save many lives, are called crash test dummies. Even though dummies can "feel" (or virtually replicate and simulate human sensory perceptions), they have the advantage of not getting hurt the way humans could. ●

Anatomy in Action

The dummies have rubber skin, aluminum skeletons, and internal electronic sensors. In tests, dummies are dressed—to reduce friction—and protected by air bags and safety belts. The force of each impact is collected by a computer located in the vehicle's back seat. In a strong impact, dummies can have their "skin" cut, but only rarely are they damaged any more than this.

SAFETY FEATURES

AIR BAG
In a collision, 10.5 to 21 gallons (40 to 80 l) of air inflate the air bag in less than a tenth of a second.

SAFETY BELT
prevents passengers from being ejected from the vehicle or from being thrown onto the steering wheel, windshield, or front seat.

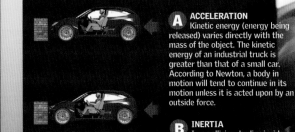

COLLISION ACCORDING TO THE LAWS OF PHYSICS
The inertial forces in a collision are enormous. Energy is neither created nor destroyed; it is only transferred. Injuries sustained in a collision are the tangible effects of energy that could not be absorbed in any other fashion.

TIME IN THOUSANDTHS OF A SECOND

0
10
20
30
40
50
54
60
70
80
84
90
100
110
150

A ACCELERATION
Kinetic energy (energy being released) varies directly with the mass of the object. The kinetic energy of an industrial truck is greater than that of a small car. According to Newton, a body in motion will tend to continue in its motion unless it is acted upon by an outside force.

B INERTIA
In a collision, bodies inside the vehicle continue to move forward, because they resist changes to their motion. Safety belts counteract this inertia and help keep the driver and passengers in their seats. Air bags reduce the chance of possible injuries during collision when the body is propelled forward and hits the dashboard.

C ENERGY ABSORPTION
Newton's laws apply to the inside of a body just as much as to the outside. When a moving head encounters an obstruction, the head and its contents tend to keep moving forward, causing the brain to strike the inside of the cranial cavity—or the spleen to collide with the abdominal cavity.

A car with a mass of 2,200 pounds (1,000 kg), moving at 60 miles per hour (100 km/h), exerts 160,000 pounds (74,000 kg) of force during a collision.

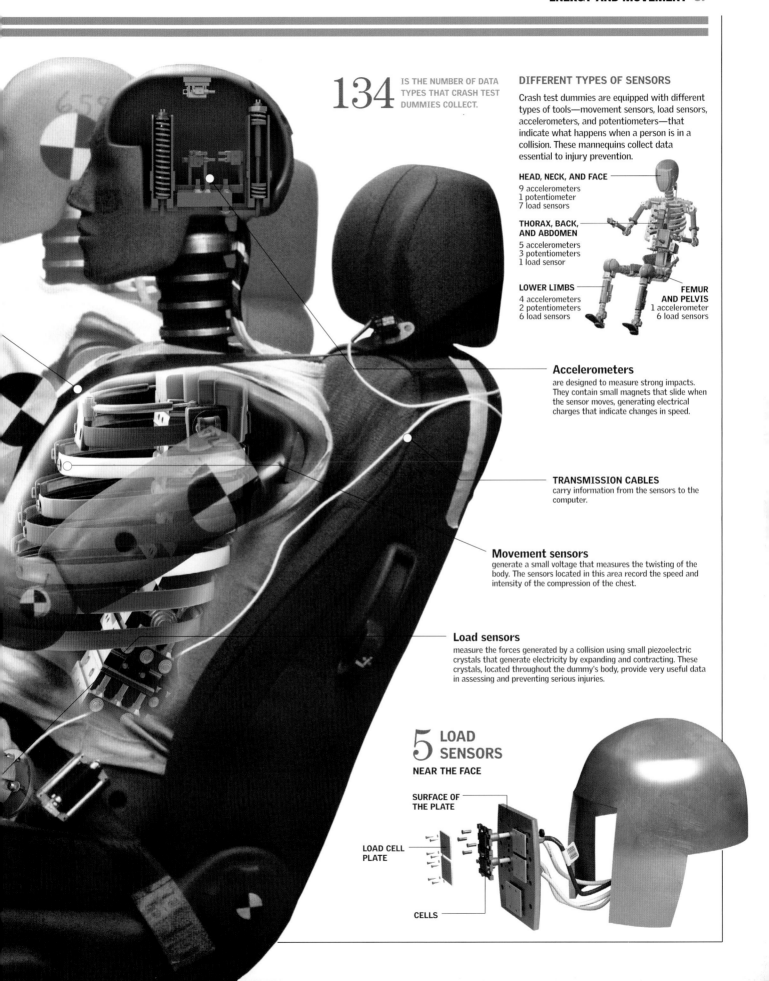

134 IS THE NUMBER OF DATA TYPES THAT CRASH TEST DUMMIES COLLECT.

DIFFERENT TYPES OF SENSORS

Crash test dummies are equipped with different types of tools—movement sensors, load sensors, accelerometers, and potentiometers—that indicate what happens when a person is in a collision. These mannequins collect data essential to injury prevention.

HEAD, NECK, AND FACE
9 accelerometers
1 potentiometer
7 load sensors

THORAX, BACK, AND ABDOMEN
5 accelerometers
3 potentiometers
1 load sensor

LOWER LIMBS
4 accelerometers
2 potentiometers
6 load sensors

FEMUR AND PELVIS
1 accelerometer
6 load sensors

Accelerometers
are designed to measure strong impacts. They contain small magnets that slide when the sensor moves, generating electrical charges that indicate changes in speed.

TRANSMISSION CABLES
carry information from the sensors to the computer.

Movement sensors
generate a small voltage that measures the twisting of the body. The sensors located in this area record the speed and intensity of the compression of the chest.

Load sensors
measure the forces generated by a collision using small piezoelectric crystals that generate electricity by expanding and contracting. These crystals, located throughout the dummy's body, provide very useful data in assessing and preventing serious injuries.

5 LOAD SENSORS
NEAR THE FACE

SURFACE OF THE PLATE

LOAD CELL PLATE

CELLS

Roller Coasters

These colossal, twisted structures provide an exhilarating and frenetic ride. They wed technology to basic and seemingly incompatible emotions, such as panic, courage, fear, joy, vertigo, and amusement. Built as if to exclusively prove Newton's theories, the science of roller coasters abounds with all his terminology: acceleration, mass, gravity, movement, and inertia. But in all this, what is really thrilling is the free fall, the attraction of the abyss. ●

Safety Details

The designers of these extreme machines take into account all possible safety factors to provide as safe an experience as possible. Riders are made to wear safety belts, and machine parts are inspected on a regular basis to prevent accidents. Joints and beams are X-rayed for flaws. Safety devices applied to the drive chain before cars reach the top prevent the train of cars from moving backward. These devices are also installed on some of the hills, where the train slows down in its climb. In the event of wind gusts and sudden decelerations, these preventive measures keep the train in place and stop it from backtracking.

Special device
is located intermittently along the chain lift. As the train prepares for its descent, this device prevents it from moving backward.

Safety device

Steel rail

Protection chain

Wheels to keep the trolley on the track
Three types of wheels are needed: upper wheels to control the train for most of the route; lower ones for use on the hills—G forces are sometimes greater than the weight of the train; and lateral wheels to prevent the train from derailing on curves.

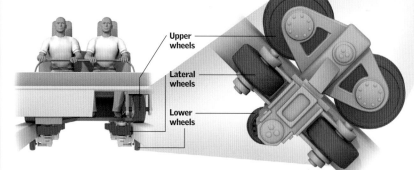

Upper wheels

Lateral wheels

Lower wheels

3

KINETIC ENERGY
is energy of motion—that is, the energy released by the train every time it descends.

K   P

128 miles per hour
(206 km/h)
is the speed reached by Kingda Ka, the highest and fastest roller coaster. It is located in New Jersey.

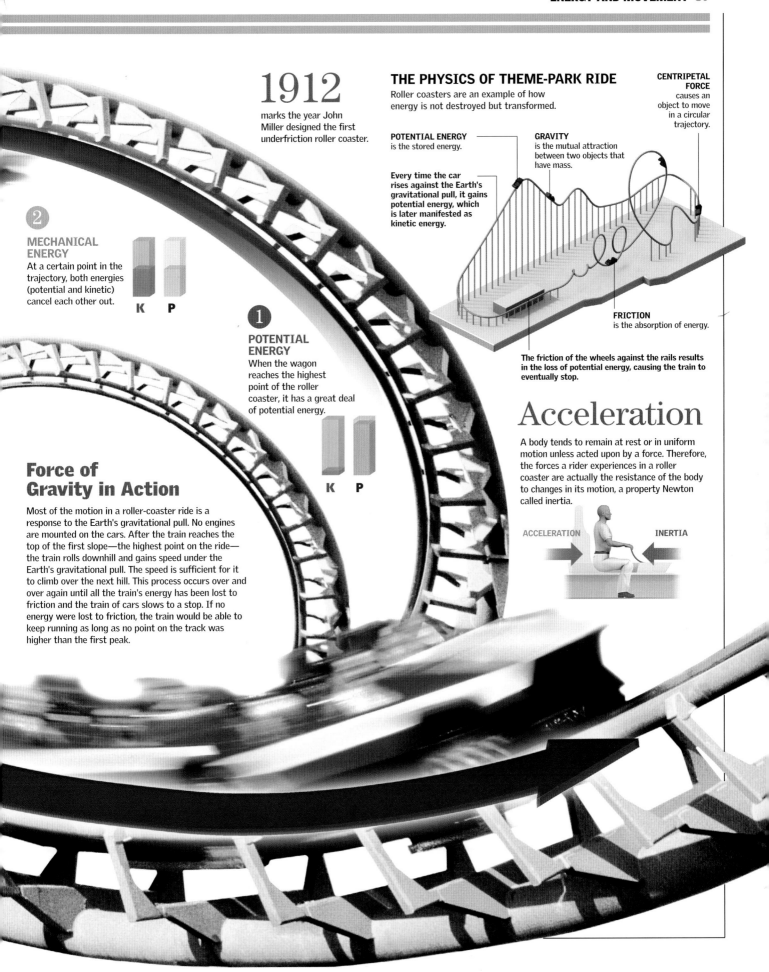

1912

marks the year John Miller designed the first underfriction roller coaster.

THE PHYSICS OF THEME-PARK RIDE

Roller coasters are an example of how energy is not destroyed but transformed.

CENTRIPETAL FORCE causes an object to move in a circular trajectory.

POTENTIAL ENERGY is the stored energy.

GRAVITY is the mutual attraction between two objects that have mass.

Every time the car rises against the Earth's gravitational pull, it gains potential energy, which is later manifested as kinetic energy.

FRICTION is the absorption of energy.

The friction of the wheels against the rails results in the loss of potential energy, causing the train to eventually stop.

2 MECHANICAL ENERGY

At a certain point in the trajectory, both energies (potential and kinetic) cancel each other out.

K   P

1 POTENTIAL ENERGY

When the wagon reaches the highest point of the roller coaster, it has a great deal of potential energy.

K   P

Force of Gravity in Action

Most of the motion in a roller-coaster ride is a response to the Earth's gravitational pull. No engines are mounted on the cars. After the train reaches the top of the first slope—the highest point on the ride—the train rolls downhill and gains speed under the Earth's gravitational pull. The speed is sufficient for it to climb over the next hill. This process occurs over and over again until all the train's energy has been lost to friction and the train of cars slows to a stop. If no energy were lost to friction, the train would be able to keep running as long as no point on the track was higher than the first peak.

Acceleration

A body tends to remain at rest or in uniform motion unless acted upon by a force. Therefore, the forces a rider experiences in a roller coaster are actually the resistance of the body to changes in its motion, a property Newton called inertia.

ACCELERATION   INERTIA

Automobiles

he first attempts at manufacturing automobiles took place in China at the end of the 17th century, although the first recorded use of an automobile dates back to 1769, when Nicolas-Joseph Cugnot created a steam-propelled car. Karl Benz gave cars their current form in 1886. Since the introduction of the Model T assembly line, automobiles have not only changed the urban and rural landscape but also, most importantly, have completely transformed modern industry. ●

On the Inside

A number of complementary systems allow the cars to function. Sophisticated electronics and state-of-the-art design make today's models veritable mechanical jewels.

AIR BAG SYSTEM
inflates several flexible bags inside the car, absorbing much of the impact that riders are subjected to during a collision.

STEERING WHEEL
activates the steering mechanism that turns the front wheels.

DIFFERENTIAL
uses a system of gears to power both drive wheels equally even when they may have different rotation speeds (when curving, for example).

WINDSHIELD
is laminated to keep it from shattering during collision.

FUEL-INJECTION SYSTEM
electronically controls the amount of fuel injected into each cylinder.

FRONT SUSPENSION
Set of springs and shock absorbers that absorbs vibrations caused by uneven terrain

AIR INTAKE
The air that enters the engine passes through a filter before mixing with the gasoline.

RADIATOR
cools down the engine's coolant.

COMPRESSOR
activates the car's air-conditioning system.

ALTERNATOR
generates the energy consumed by the car's electrical devices.

ENGINE
Modern engines use fuel efficiently—consuming and polluting less than ever—and they can provide high power even with relatively small engines.

MASTER BRAKE CYLINDER
Activated by the pedal, it applies hydraulic pressure to the brake calipers, causing them to grip the wheels.

GEARBOX
Series of gears used to adjust the motor's speed of revolution to that of the drive wheels

DRIVE SHAFT
Extension from the transmission connecting the gearbox to the drive wheels in cars with rear-wheel drive

CATALYTIC CONVERTER
modifies the harmful components of exhaust gases into less harmful emissions.

1769

CUGNOT
built the first steam-propelled automobile. This vehicle reached about two miles per hour (3 km/h).

1883

DAIMLER
equipped a carriage with the first gasoline engine.

1899

RENAULT
Covered and with an internal steering wheel

1901

OLDSMOBILE
The first car produced in series in the United States

1913

FORD T
In 1917, Henry Ford used an assembly line to manufacture this car.

1934

CITRÖEN
The front-wheel drive is introduced.

How the Engine Works

The development of cars began with the invention of the internal combustion engine. Its basic principle—the four-stroke engine created by the German Nikolaus Otto—has continued to be used to this day.

FIRST STROKE: INTAKE

1 The **piston** descends, creating suction

2 The **intake valve** opens.

3 A mixture of air and gas enters the **cylinder.**

SECOND STROKE: COMPRESSION

1 The **intake valve** closes.

2 The **piston rises.**

3 The mixture of air and gas is compressed into a more reduced space.

THIRD STROKE: POWER STROKE

1 At the end of the trajectory, the **spark plug** generates an electrical spark.

2 The mixture ignites, creating great pressure that pushes the piston down.

3 The force transmitted through the **piston shaft** causes the **crankshaft** to turn.

FOURTH STROKE: EXHAUST STROKE

1 The **escape valve** opens.

3 Once the piston reaches the top of its stroke, the **cycle** begins again.

2 The **piston** starts to rise, pushing along the hot gases.

BODYWORK
is designed to deform progressively in order to absorb as much energy as possible during a collision.

REAR SUSPENSION

MUFFLER
reduces the noise produced by gases as they exit the exhaust pipe.

WHEEL RIM
is made out of a lightweight alloy to lower the weight of the wheel.

TIRE
has a low profile, improving stability during fast turns.

DISK BRAKE
A brake pad attached to the wheel, it is gripped by the calipers when the brake pedal is depressed.

EXHAUST PIPE
expels engine exhaust away from the vehicle.

1936
BEETLE
The first Volkswagen car was designed by Porsche at Hitler's request.

1948
FERRARI
The company presents its first street car, the 166 Sport.

1954
MERCEDES-BENZ 300 SL
Known as "Seagull Wings," it was the first car with a fuel-injection engine.

1955
FIAT 600
This popular compact city car is produced in Italy.

1964
CADILLAC DE VILLE
A spacious convertible, it was the ultimate in automobile luxury of its time.

2007
TOYOTA HYBRID X
A concept car with a sunroof, LED headlights, swiveling rear seats, and drive-by-wire controls

Trains

Although rail transportation dates back to ancient Greece (6th century BC), this technology has only recently (beginning of the 19th century) been used to its full potential. Trains were essential to the Industrial Revolution, and during their almost 200 years of existence, they have evolved into increasingly fast models. Some—such as the TGV (France), the Shinkansen (Japan), the AVE (Spain), and the Intercity 125 (United Kingdom)—travel faster than 185 miles per hour (300 km/h). ●

LOCOMOTIVE
Equipped with powerful electric engines, the TGV's locomotives can travel at high speed even while climbing hills. Because the train has a locomotive at each end, the locomotive does not need to be repositioned before a trip in the other direction.

AIR DAM

357.16 miles per hour
(574.8 km/h)
IN A TEST RUN, A TGV REACHED THIS SPEED IN 2007, SETTING A NEW RAIL SPEED RECORD.

How It Works

High speeds were achieved because of aerodynamic designs, lighter and more powerful locomotives, and exclusive-use railway routes.

SOURCE OF ENERGY
Locomotives get 25,000 volts of electric energy from power cables through a pantograph, a mobile mechanism that travels with the train and keeps the electrical circuit alive.

Suspended power cable

Collector

ELECTRIC CURRENT

Springs

Flexible arms

Piston

CONTROL CABIN

EMERGENCY EXIT

RÉSEAU FERRÉ DE FRANCE ALSTOM SNCF

02

84 004

DRIVE
Each wheel has an independent electric engine.

RAILS
The principle of rail travel has remained essentially the same for the past 150 years.

Control cable

Electric motor

Rail

Rail head

Rail web

Rail foot

Concrete or wooden sleeper

Drive wheel

Axis

Rail clip

Motorcycles

hese agile vehicles are commonly used in both transportation and racing. The first motorcycle was invented in 1885. During the 20th century, motorcycles became a symbol of youthfulness and rebellion. The first motorcycles were used for mail distribution. Special motorcycles were then manufactured for urban environments, racing, and tourism. Models with even faster and more powerful engines were also invented for those looking for extreme experiences on two wheels.

Some Types of Motorcycles

WINDSHIELD
On some models, windshields can be adjusted according to the driver's height.

MIRRORS

ENDURANCE
All-terrain motorcycles. They are used in the famous Paris-Dakar race.

HEADLIGHTS
Two wide, shining multifaceted reflectors

SCOOTER
Small vehicles are useful for urban transportation because they are very maneuverable and economical.

RACE
Very powerful and equipped with the latest technology. They are used for high-level competitions.

WHEELS
are made of aluminum, which make them light and resistant to damage.

BRAKES
A dual braking system balances the front and rear brakes.

History

STREET
With small engines (125 cc and 150 cc), these are economical, high-performance motorcycles.

TTHE FIRST
Built on a wooden frame by Gottlieb Daimler in Germany

SINGLE
It has a 1.75 HP engine and a chain transmission, and it can reach 25 miles per hour (40 km/h).

ROAD
Very comfortable and designed to travel great distances on paved roads

1885   1901

Motorcycle for Tourism or Adventure

➤ This model is one of the most versatile; it adjusts to mountain paths as well as to roads. Equipped with electronic innovations and a powerful engine, it is comfortable and can even carry loads.

CONTROL PANEL
is digital and has a liquid quartz display with an odometer, a clock, and a fuel gauge.

SEAT

137 miles per hour
(220 km/h) km/h

ENGINE
Two-cylinder, four-stroke engine

BAGGAGE COMPARTMENT

TURN SIGNAL

MUFFLER

ENGINE

GEARBOX

Engine capacity	61 cubic inches (996 cu cm)
Cylinders	V2
Valves	8
Gearbox	6 speeds

FUEL TANK
is made of aluminum and has a capacity of 6.6 gallons (25 l).

FRAME
is dual-beam and made out of aluminum. It uses a central shock absorber to support the rear of the vehicle.

SINGLE RACING
An adjustable front suspension and an experimental electronic ignition have been added.

POWERPLUS
With a sidecar (for passengers), it is the first motorcycle to use an engine with lateral valves.

PRINCE
With 20 HP and three speeds, it reaches more than 46 miles per hour (75 km/h).

CHIEF
In the postwar period, it was popular with police in New York City.

HONDA GL 1500
A motorcycle is ideal for couples. It has a powerful engine and is almost as comfortable as an automobile.

KAWASAKI
Its striking design highlights this model's joining of technology and aesthetics.

1914 1916 1928 1946 1988 2007

Bicycles

This two-wheel vehicle is not only a healthy, environmentally friendly, and economical means of transportation, but it is also extraordinarily efficient! Up to 99 percent of the energy a cyclist transfers to the pedals reaches the wheels. In fact, it is the most efficient load-bearing vehicle. Bicycles have played important sociocultural roles, giving rural and urban workers more mobility and symbolizing freedom during the first feminist movements. ●

How the Gear Shifter Works

Most chain wheels have 48 teeth. A complete turn moves 48 chain joints.

1
On flat terrain, the 12-toothed gear should be used, putting the bicycle in high gear.

2 By turning the chain wheel a quarter rotation, both the gear and the wheel make a complete turn.

3
When ascending, the 24-tooth gear should be selected, putting the bicycle into low gear.

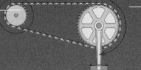

4 With every half turn of the chain wheel, the gear makes one complete turn. In this way, the force thus transmitted doubles without any effort on the part of the cyclist. In other words, this force only travels half the distance every time the chain wheel completes one rotation.

TRACK BICYCLE

Aerodynamic design for racing

They do not have gears.

They do not have brakes.

Made of aluminum and compound materials, such as carbon fibers and epoxy resins

MOUNTAIN BIKE

Reinforced frame. It can withstand the wear and tear of racing.

Multiple gear ratios

Front and rear suspensions, which absorb irregularities in the terrain

Articulated frame

GEAR SELECTOR
uses the derailleur to select from the different speeds.

HANDLEBARS
allow the cyclist to guide the bicycle by changing the direction of the front wheel.

BRAKE CABLE

BRAKES
apply force to the rims and are activated from the handlebars by means of levers and cables.

FORK
connects the front wheel to the handlebars. Some models have shock absorbers.

SPOKES
They connect the rim to the hub, adding structural rigidity to the wheel with only a negligible addition of weight.

History

The first bicycle did not have pedals; it was propelled by the feet.

1769

Karl von Drais de Sauerbrun invented the *draisienne*, which had greater separation between the wheels, the handlebars, and the seat.

1818

Pierre Lallement added pedals connected to the front wheel, which was larger than the rear on

1865

SPROCKETS
Set of gears with diameters that differ from those of the drive gear. They allow the wheel to turn at different speeds as the cyclist pedals at the same pace and level of effort.

REAR BRAKE

REAR DERAILLEUR keeps the chain tensed.

50%
of the world's bicycles are in China.

FRAME is composed of metallic tubes welded together.

PEDALS act as levers, making the chain wheel rotate.

CHAIN WHEEL

der l the ame.

James Starley invented the chain-driven safety bicycle with wheels of the same diameter.

Bicycles were given their current shape. The derailleur was patented.

The three-speed English bicycle was introduced along with some other novel designs.

New materials, such as acrylic, stainless steel, and carbon fiber, have come into general use.

37   1885   1896   1950   Today

Boats and Ships

One of the first means of transportation invented, boats made it possible for people to overcome the obstacles posed by water. Although boats and larger vessels called ships have undergone many technological advances, they all depend upon the flotation principle discovered by Archimedes. Boats and ships are commonly used in trade, recreation, and military operations.

Freighters

are used to transport dry products. The model shown was first built in the 1970s, and it is still used today, though with many technological improvements.

Helm

acts as a steering wheel. When it is turned, the ship changes direction.

STRAIGHT RUDDER

Water

The ship moves straight ahead.

LEFT RUDDER

Water

The ship turns left.

RIGHT RUDDER

Water

The ship turns right.

Propeller (screw)

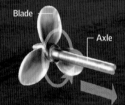

1 Driven by the engines, the propeller turns.

2 The water is pushed backward.

3 The force of reaction pushes the ship forward.

Blade

Axle

Flag indicating the ship's country of origin

Awning

Lifeboat

MACHINERY ROOM
has the diesel engines that provide the power to propel the ship.

DOUBLE HULL
is where the fuel tanks, drinkable water, and ballast tanks are located.

Main deck

Lower deck

Orlop deck

HOLD

The History of Boats and Ships

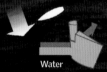

Wind

SAILING SHIPS. 15TH CENTURY.
The wind was the first propulsive force used. Sailing ships were widely used for journeys of exploration.

The paddle wheel is driven by a steam engine.

STERNWHEELERS. Beginning of the 19th century. Oldest ship propelled by an engine. The blades of the paddle wheel, acting like oars, cause the boat to move.

Propeller   Engine

WITH A PROPELLER. Since 1830. The invention of the propeller, or screw, allowed, at a small expense of energy, the transportation of extremely heavy loads at higher speeds.

BRIDGE
The ship and all
onboard activities are
directed from here.

DECK CRANES
Each is controlled by an
operator from a cabin.

HULL
Hollow structure made
of welded steel sheets,
its interior is divided into
floors or decks.

WHY IT FLOATS

The steel hull is denser
than the water, but
because it has air in its
interior, it floats.

The water pushes the
boat upward.

STACK
bears the flag
of the naval
company.

LOADING HATCHES
This boat is a mixed
freighter because it can
store merchandise in the
hold as well as in
containers.

Folded deck
cranes

Ship's flag

WINDLASS
is used to drop and
raise the anchor.

Hatch
cover

Forecastle

Handrail

ANCHOR

WATERLINE

Air   Propeller

Air-cushion vehicle

HOVERCRAFT. Since 1960.
It uses propellers that produce an air
cushion below the boat. Some ferries
use this flotation system.

Sailboats

Very early in history, human beings used wind to carry their vessels along, covering long distances on water. This was necessary for trade and conquest, because it permitted, at much less effort than would otherwise have been necessary, the transportation of large quantities of merchandise and troops. Except for a few zones in the Indian Ocean, sailboats are now generally used for sport and recreation. The invention of triangular and trapezoidal sails that not only harness wind power but also exploit other physical phenomenon made boats easier to maneuver.

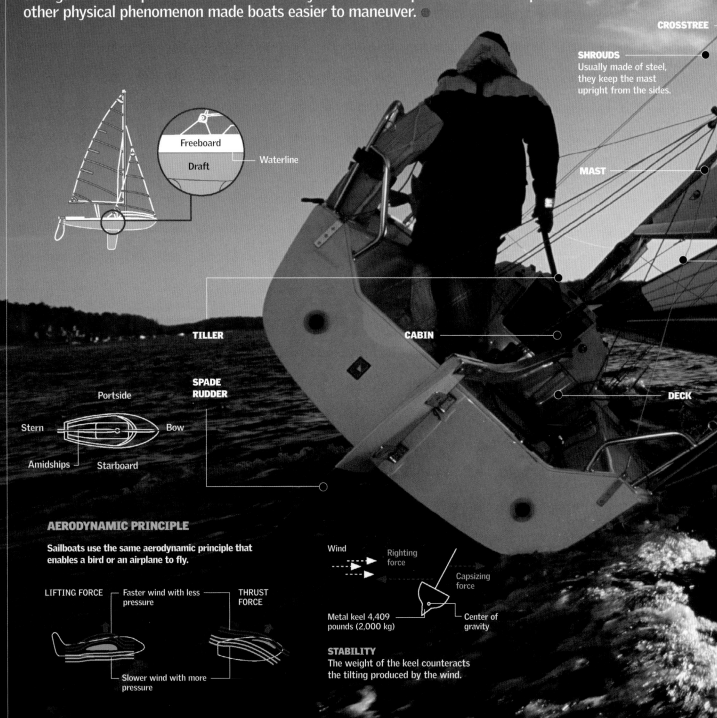

CROSSTREE

SHROUDS
Usually made of steel, they keep the mast upright from the sides.

MAST

Freeboard

Draft — Waterline

TILLER

CABIN

DECK

SPADE RUDDER

Portside

Stern   Bow

Amidships — Starboard

AERODYNAMIC PRINCIPLE

Sailboats use the same aerodynamic principle that enables a bird or an airplane to fly.

LIFTING FORCE — Faster wind with less pressure   THRUST FORCE

Slower wind with more pressure

Wind   Righting force

Capsizing force

Metal keel 4,409 pounds (2,000 kg)   Center of gravity

STABILITY
The weight of the keel counteracts the tilting produced by the wind.

TYPES OF RIGGING
The mast, boom, forestays, and shrouds are together called rigging.

SPORTS SAILBOATS

Cat

Sloop

Yawl

Ketch

Cat

Schooner

CLIPPER

TELLTALE
Attached to the shroud and stay, it is used to indicate the direction of the wind.

MAINSAIL

BOOM

THE WIND
propels sailboats. Sailors distinguish between three types of wind.

RELATIVE
is generated as the sailboat moves. This wind goes from the bow to the stern.

APPARENT
is the disparity between the relative and real winds.

REAL
is what we commonly call wind.

VENTURI EFFECT
is produced in the so-called "funnel," where the wind gains speed as the space between the sails diminishes.

Wind

Jib

Venturi Effect

Mainsail

COURSES
It is possible to sail in all directions except against the wind.

TO STARBOARD

TO PORT

The Venturi effect is produced. The shape of the sails is important.

The force of the thrust causes the sailboat to move. The surface of the sail is important.

DIRECTION OF THE WIND

Close-hauled

Close-hauled

Close reach

Close reach

Beam reach

DEAD ZONE 60°

Beam reach

Broad reach

Broad reach

Aft quartering

Aft quartering

Running

Balloons

The use of balloons constitutes the first successful application of a flight technique developed by humans. Although the first recorded balloon flight was carried out by the Montgolfier brothers, the Chinese used unmanned balloons for military communication in the 2nd century AD. Because balloons are carried along by the wind, the pilot has a difficult time following an exact course or returning to the place of origin. Forgotten by the beginning of the 20th century, balloons have experienced a revival since the 1960s and are now used for sport and recreation.

WHY THEY FLY
Thermal differences enable balloons to fly. Certain gases and hot air are lighter than atmospheric air.

HELIUM

PRESSURE, WEIGHT, AND HEIGHT
The gases are located at different heights.

Lower weight and higher pressure: greater height

Higher weight and lower pressure: lower height

GAS BALLOONS
are mostly used in unmanned meteorological missions. They are usually filled with hydrogen or helium, both light gases.

HOT-AIR BALLOONS
As the air heats up, it expands and becomes less dense.

Cold air is heavier and tends to descend.

Hot air is lighter and rises.

MANEUVERING IN THE AIR
Only the upward and downward movements of balloons can be controlled. To move horizontally, balloons use wind and particular air currents.

The strength and direction of wind vary with altitude.

High-altitude winds

By rising or descending to various altitudes, balloonists can control the course and speed of their balloons.

Strong, high-altitude winds

Weak winds

The wind never tips a balloon but pushes it along and sometimes makes it spin.

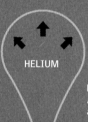

A propane gas burner heats up the air inside the balloon. As the air molecules are heated, the air expands and becomes less dense.

When the balloon is filled with air that is less dense than the atmospheric air surrounding it, the balloon rises.

ROZIER BALLOONS
are a combination of helium and hot-air balloons.

The balloonist can change altitude by controlling air temperature.

It also allows for long trips at high altitudes.

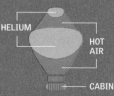

HELIUM

HOT AIR

CABIN

BREITLING ORBITER 3
In 1999, Brian Jones (Britain) and Bertrand Piccard (Switzerland) flew nonstop around the world in this Rozier balloon. The trip lasted about 19 days and 22 hours, during which the balloon was kept at an altitude that would have been too high for hot-air balloons.

180 feet (55 m)

THE FLIGHT OF THE BREITLING ORBITER
36,000 feet (11,000 m)

MOUNT EVEREST
29,035 feet (8,850 m)

RIP PANELS

SEGMENTS
There are balloons with 8, 16, or even 24 segments.

ENVELOPE
Made of nylon or polyester coated in durable and low-weight polyurethane (to keep air from escaping), it contains the heated air.

SKIRT
Some balloons have a skirt made of nonflammable material that prevents the nylon from catching fire during the inflation process.

The lower part is open so the burner can heat the air.

Although the balloon is open at the bottom, the hot air does not escape because it accumulates in the upper part of the balloon.

Components

CONTROL FLAP
In big balloons, it is used to control the altitude.

While it is shut, the hot air stays inside the balloon, where it maintains its lighter density, causing the balloon to ascend.

SHUT

When the valve is open, some hot air escapes, lowering the density of the air inside the balloon and causing the craft to descend.

OPEN

To land, the balloon must be nearly deflated.

BURNERS
use propane, just like the portable stoves used in camping.

GONDOLA FOR THE PILOT AND PASSENGERS

Dirigibles

Because of the difficulty inherent in steering a balloon, several methods of navigation, including wings and oars, were attempted. All these methods were unsuccessful until Henri Giffard added an engine to a balloon, turning it into a dirigible. However, it was Ferdinand von Zeppelin who in 1900 gave dirigibles their rigid structure and definitive shape. Dirigibles were then used to transport passengers, but now they are used almost exclusively for advertising. Many companies are considering using them to transport cargo, because dirigibles travel much faster than boats or trucks and can lift and carry up to 500 tons. ●

656,000 cubic feet (200,000 cu m)

was the volume of gas contained in 16 compartments.

Over time, hydrogen, an inflammable gas, was replaced by helium, which is nonflammable.

THE STRUCTURE
Made of aluminum, it was rigid and covered by a thick cotton fabric.

RUDDER

ENGINES
They had four diesel engines.

How Dirigibles Fly

WORKING PRINCIPLE
They were lifted by helium or hydrogen. These gases, being less dense than air in the lower atmosphere, caused the airship to float upward to less dense regions.

1 The gas chambers were filled up with hydrogen, and the dirigible began to rise

2 Propellers driven by diesel engines were used for horizontal movement.

The Hindenburg

▶ was the largest dirigible (number 108) to leave the Zeppelin production lines. In 1937, as the Hindenburg was practicing landing maneuvers, it burst into flames. Since then, dirigibles have not been used to transport passengers commercially.

Builder	**Zeppelin Shipyard**
Speed	**84 miles per hour (135 km/h)**
Capacity	**70 passengers**
Crew	**15 people**

FERDINAND VON ZEPPELIN
German aeronaut.
He had been dreaming of flying his own dirigible since 1873 but did not manage to do so until 1900. Ten years later, his airships started to transport passengers commercially.

THE DECK
had two floors. It included passenger cabins, a restaurant, a lounge, a reading room, a bar, and a smoking lounge.

THE GONDOLA
Only crew members could enter it. The movements of the dirigible were controlled from here.

3 Dirigibles had lateral fins that, when tilted downward, caused them to descend.

Airplanes

W ithin a century, airplanes have not only fulfilled humanity's ancient wish to fly but also have become a means of transportation used by many people and can quickly cover great distances. Even though the earliest models—made of wood, fabric, and steel—have evolved into huge jets capable of carrying hundreds of passengers over oceans as well as into supersonic military aircraft, all planes are governed by the same physical laws.

Held Up by the Air

The upper side of an airplane's wing is curved, but the lower side is straight. This design makes the air flowing above the wing travel farther than the air below, thereby increasing its speed. As a result, the pressure of the air above decreases, and the wing is supported in part by the pressure of the air below it. If the flow of air is interrupted or is inadequate, the airplane loses lift and can stall.

Propulsion

In order to fly, airplanes must be constantly propelled forward. The most efficient system of aerial propulsion uses the expansive force of hot gases created by burning compressed air.

1 The air enters the engine and passes through a compressor, increasing its pressure.

2 The newly compressed air is mixed with fuel and burned. Its temperature increases to about 1,300° F (700° C), creating high-pressure gases that escape through the exhaust nozzles.

3 As the hot gases escape, pushing the aircraft forward, they turn turbines that power the compressor and, in some engines, the turbofans, thereby restarting the cycle.

4 The gases escape from the turbine at high speed and push the aircraft forward.

SUBSONIC ENGINES

Turboprop

Part of the energy from the jet engine is used to turn a propeller, which provides propulsion.

Combustion chamber

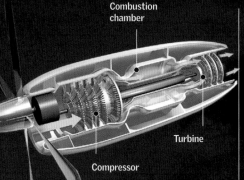

Turbine

Compressor

Cold air
Hot air

Turbofan

Any excess air that enters the engine flows on both sides of the turbine without burning, thus making the engine quieter, more efficient, and more economical.

Combustion chamber

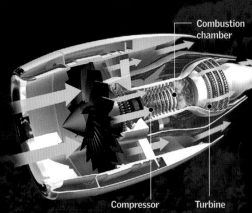

The blades draw in air

Compressor   Turbine

Mach

is a unit equivalent to the speed of sound. This speed depends on the temperature and other factors, but one Mach is generally considered to be 761 miles per hour (1,225 km/h).

In Flight

Once airborne, a pilot controls an airplane's direction and altitude with movable surfaces controlled from the cockpit.

RUDDER

is controlled with pedals; it turns the nose of the airplane to the right or the left. The rudder usually works in coordination with the ailerons.

ELEVATOR

lifts or lowers the airplane's nose, causing the aircraft to change altitude.

FLAPS

are extendible panels used during takeoff and landing. When they extend, they increase the surface area of the wings, thereby increasing the amount of lift generated and enabling the aircraft to either takeoff or fly at even lower speeds.

AILERONS

cause the airplane to roll during flight. They are movable panels that rotate the plane on its long axis, allowing the plane to bank into a turn. The ailerons are activated by the control wheel or stick.

SUPERSONIC ENGINES

Turbojet

has a second combustion chamber that, when activated, burns gases at high pressure, thereby creating additional thrust. It is used in military airplanes.

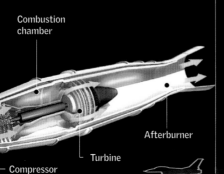

Combustion chamber

Afterburner

Turbine

Compressor

HYPERSONIC ENGINES

Scramjets

are a type of experimental engine designed to operate at and above Mach 6. The air goes into the engine with such force that the aircraft requires neither turbines nor compressors but only two burners.

Intake

Combustion chamber

Helicopters

C ompared to airplanes, helicopters are not only a much more complex means of transportation, but they are also accompanied by higher manufacturing, operational, and maintenance expenses. They are slower and have shorter range; they also possess lower load-bearing capacities than fixed-wing aircrafts, but all these disadvantages are offset by their great maneuverability. Helicopters can hover, remaining motionless in the air, and they can even rotate in place. They can also take off and land vertically using any reasonably large, level spot that is twice as large as the space the helicopter occupies. ●

Twin Rotors

Most large helicopters use two main rotors to double the lift generated. They can transport heavy loads and considerable numbers of passengers. These helicopters can be used as ambulances; they can also be used in search, rescue, and logistical missions.

How It Flies

THE ROTOR

has blades that generate the lift necessary for the helicopter to rise and move from place to place. The pitch of the blades is controlled by a swashplate connected to two control columns. The swashplate can move upward, downward, or at an incline between the columns, holding the blades at various levels of pitch. The swashplate also moves the control axes that change the pitch of the entire rotor.

THE BLADES

have an aerodynamic profile similar to that of airplanes. Their pitch can be changed to vary the lift they produce for different types of flight.

Rotor disk
It comprises the blades and the rotor shaft and rotates with them.

Rotor shaft

Rod controlling the degree of inclination

Swashplate
does not revolve, but it travels up and down and tilts on joints that connect it to the control column.

PITOT TUBE
records the atmospheric pressure and calculates height and speeds.

HOVERING

The rotor blades are not pitched relative to the rotor shaft. This creates a lift equal to the weight of the machine and causes the helicopter to remain suspended in the air, moving neither forward nor backward.

Shaft
Blades
Swashplate

FORWARD

When the swashplate moves forward, the rotor disk tilts forward, increasing the lift generated by the back of the rotor to push the helicopter forward.

VERTICAL FLIGHT

When the swashplate is raised, the pitch of each blade increases, which generates more lift and causes the helicopter to ascend. When descending, the swashplate is lowered, causing each blade to decrease pitch and generate less lift.

BACKWARD

When the swashplate is moved backward, the rotor disk tilts backward, increasing the lift generated by the front of the rotor to push the helicopter backward.

CH-47 Chinook

Its history started in the 1950s, when the American army developed it as a means of transportation for troops and crews. Its engines, design, and internal systems have continually improved.

Type	Tandom-rotor transport
Crew	2 pilots + 1 mechanic
Range with maximum load	621 miles (300 km)
Speed at sea level	186 miles per hour (300 km/h)
Maximum altitude	11,480 feet (3,500 m)
Engine	Two 3,750 HP turbo engines
Empty weight	21,460 pounds (9,736 kg)
Maximum weight	50,270 pounds (22,800 kg)

TAIL ROTOR

prevents the machine from rotating around itself.

Attack
AH-64
Apache

Passenger
Sikorsky S-61

Tiltrotors
V-22 Osprey

Load-bearing
Sikorsky Sky Crane

Futuristic
Sikorsky RAH-66. Comanche,
almost undetectable by radars

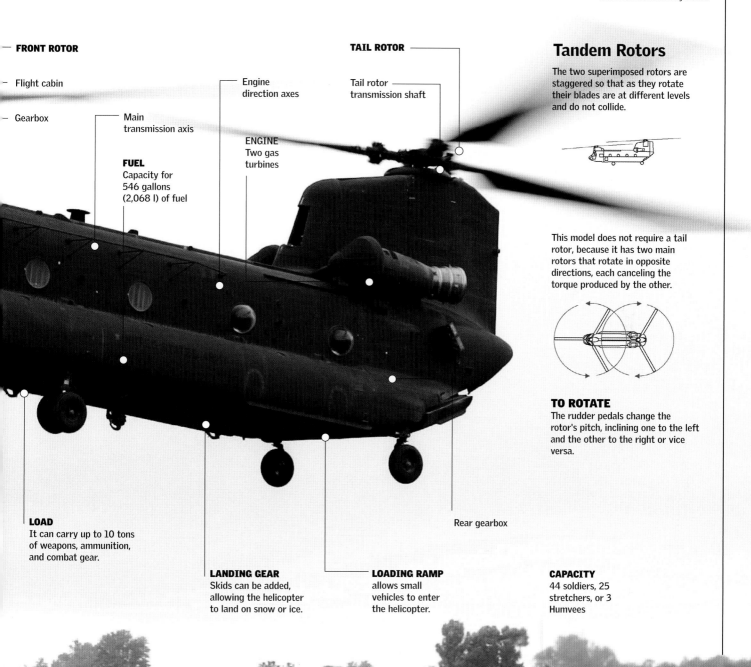

— **FRONT ROTOR**

— Flight cabin

— Gearbox

**Main
transmission axis**

FUEL
Capacity for
546 gallons
(2,068 l) of fuel

ENGINE
Two gas
turbines

Engine
direction axes

TAIL ROTOR

Tail rotor
transmission shaft

LOAD
It can carry up to 10 tons
of weapons, ammunition,
and combat gear.

LANDING GEAR
Skids can be added,
allowing the helicopter
to land on snow or ice.

Rear gearbox

LOADING RAMP
allows small
vehicles to enter
the helicopter.

Tandem Rotors

The two superimposed rotors are
staggered so that as they rotate
their blades are at different levels
and do not collide.

This model does not require a tail
rotor, because it has two main
rotors that rotate in opposite
directions, each canceling the
torque produced by the other.

TO ROTATE
The rudder pedals change the
rotor's pitch, inclining one to the left
and the other to the right or vice
versa.

CAPACITY
44 soldiers, 25
stretchers, or 3
Humvees

Hydrogen

S ome people consider hydrogen the energy source of the future and predict that in the short term it will gain widespread use in place of fossil fuels. The hydrogen is combined with oxygen to release energy to generate electricity. Among the advantages of hydrogen-based energy are its very low pollution level (the byproduct of the reaction is water vapor) and its inexhaustibility (it can be recycled and reused). Disadvantages include the complications inherent in handling pure hydrogen, its costs, and the wide-scale conversion that would be necessary for petroleum-fueled engines and systems.

O

H

Fuel Cells

➤ produce electricity from the energy released during the chemical reaction of hydrogen and oxygen. The engine converts the electrical energy into mechanical energy.

Fuel-cell pack

200 is the average number of hydrogen cells a car engine needs.

Flow plate

Hydrogen and oxygen circulate through the channels of their respective plates on either side of the electrolytic membrane.

Cooling cell

The cooling cell should be refrigerated because the reaction produced in the cell generates heat.

Separator

Flow plate

Cathode

is the electrode in contact with the oxygen atoms and the place where water vapor forms.

Catalyst

Electrolyte

is a cell through which the hydrogen nuclei pass before reaching the cathode. It does not allow electrons, which flow through the external circuit (electricity), to pass.

0.7 volt

is the voltage generated by a single fuel cell. This energy can scarcely light one lightbulb, but tens or hundreds of cells can be joined together to increase this voltage.

Anode

The electrode in contact with hydrogen atoms.

Catalyst

causes the hydrogen nuclei to separate from their electrons.

The Cleanest Car

The latest hydrogen-fueled models can travel up to 100 miles per hour (160 km/h) and have a range between 170 and 250 miles (270 and 400 km), depending on whether liquid or compressed hydrogen is used.

Hydrogen canister valve

Starter battery

Converter

From direct current to alternating current

Air compressor

Air filter

Radiator

cools down the cells.

Fuel cells

use hydrogen and oxygen to generate electricity.

Electric engine

causes the car wheels to move.

Fuel pipes

carry hydrogen from the tank to the cells.

Exhaust pipe

releases the water vapor produced by the process.

Tank

is designed to store compressed or liquid hydrogen.

Glass fiber

Aluminum

Carbon fiber

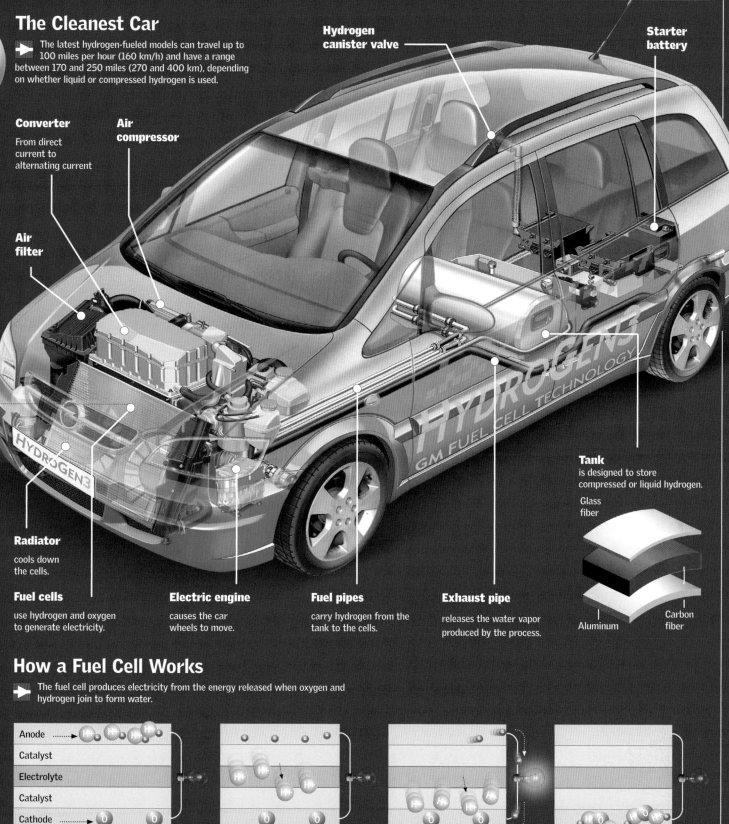

How a Fuel Cell Works

The fuel cell produces electricity from the energy released when oxygen and hydrogen join to form water.

| Anode |
| Catalyst |
| Electrolyte |
| Catalyst |
| Cathode |

1 Hydrogen collects at the anode and oxygen at the cathode. The catalyst separates the hydrogen electrons from their nuclei.

2 Hydrogen nuclei cross the electrolytic layer without their electrons.

3 Electrons, which cannot cross the electrolytic layer, flow through the circuit until they reach the cathode, thereby producing electric current.

4 The byproducts of the process are water and heat. The reaction continues as long as fuel is supplied.

Glossary

Acid

An acid is any chemical compound that, dissolved in water, produces a solution with a pH lower than 7.

Aerodynamics

Branch of fluid mechanics that studies interactions between solid bodies in motion through a fluid surrounding them. In solving an aerodynamic problem, it is necessary to calculate properties of the fluid-such as speed, direction, pressure, density, and temperature-in relation to the position of the object through time.

Aerostatic Balloon

A flying device with a gondola for passengers attached to an envelope of lightweight, impermeable material. This envelope assumes a roughly spherical shape and is filled with gas of lower density than air; this situation creates a lift strong enough to overcome its weight.

Alkaline

Low-density, colored, soft metals that react easily with halogens to form ionic salts, as well as with water to form strong hydroxide bases. All have just one electron in their valence shell, which they tend to lose, forming singly charged ions.

Allotropy

Property certain chemical elements possess that enables them to be classified under different molecular structures or according to different physical properties. For example, oxygen can either exist as molecular oxygen (O_2) or ozone (O_3). Other examples are phosphorus, which can either occur as white or red phosphorous (P_4), or carbon, which can occur as either graphite or diamond. For an element to be defined as an allotrope, its different molecular structures must exist within the same physical state.

Alternator

Machine that transforms mechanical energy into electrical energy by using induction to generate an alternating current. Alternators are based on the principle that in a conductor subjected to a variable magnetic field, an induced voltage will be created, voltage whose polarity depends on the direction of the field and whose value depends on the flux crossing it. An alternator has two fundamental parts—the inductor, which creates the magnetic field, and the conductor, which passes through the lines of force of the field.

Ampere

Is the measure of the intensity of an electrical current. It is a basic unit of the International System of Units. The ampere is a constant current which—if maintained between two parallel conductors of infinite length but negligible circular cross section and placed three feet (1 m) apart in a vacuum—would produce a force equivalent to 2×10^{-7} newtons per meter of length. It is represented by the symbol A.

Anode

Positive electrode in an electrolytic cell, toward which the negative ions, or anions, move inside the electrolyte. In the case of thermionic valves, electric sources, batteries, and so on, the anode is the electrode or terminal with greater potential.

Atomic Bomb

Fission weapon whose great destructive power comes from the release of high-energy neutrons.

Baryon

Baryon is a hadron formed by three quarks that are held together by a strong nuclear interaction. The proton and neutron belong to this group.

Base

Substance that, in an aqueous solution, donates OH^- ions. Bases and acids are diametrically opposed. The generalized concept of pH is used for both acids and bases.

Bond

Union between atoms that form a compound or the force that keeps two chemical entities together.

Cathode

Negative electrode of an electrolytic cell, toward which the positive ions, or cations, move.

Coal

Combustible, black mineral of organic origin. It tends to be located under a layer of slate and over a layer of sand. It is believed that most coal was formed during the Carboniferous Era (280 to 345 million years ago).

Coil

Variable number of loops of an electrically conductive material wound around an empty, prismatic, or cylindrical core.

Connecting Rod

Part connected at one end to a piston, which moves in a straight line, and at the other end to a crankshaft, crank, or wheel to transform a linear reciprocating motion into rotational motion. Connecting rods are basic elements of today's internal combustion engines.

Convection

One of the three forms of heat transfer, it is produced by mass transfer between regions of disparate temperatures. Convection takes place only in fluids. When a fluid is heated, it becomes less dense and rises. As it rises it is displaced by lower-temperature fluid that, in turn, is heated, thus repeating the cycle.

Coulomb

Amount of charge that one ampere carries in one second. A coulomb is 6.28×10^{18} times the charge of an electron.

Crankshaft

Shaft that contains a series of cranks to which connecting rods are attached.

Dynamics

In physics, the part of mechanics that deals with the study of the motions of bodies subjected to force.

Dynamo

Direct-current generator used to transform mechanical energy into electrical energy.

Electric Motor

Transforms electrical energy into mechanical energy, which can be direct or alternating currents (DC or AC).

Electrical Conductor

A body is considered an electrical conductor if, when placed in contact with an electrically charged body, it transmits electricity to all points of its surface.

Electricity

Phenomenon produced by particles with positive or negative charge, at rest or in motion. Also, the subdiscipline of physics that studies electrical phenomena.

Electrolytic Cell

A device using electrical current to break down bodies called electrolytes. Electrolytes can be acids, bases, or salts. The dissociation process that takes place in the electrolytic cell is called electrolysis.

Fuse

Easily meltable metal wire or plate placed in electrical assemblies to interrupt excessive current flow by melting.

Fusibility

Property, possessed by many bodies, of changing state from solid to liquid when heated.

Gamma Rays

Electromagnetic radiation that is generally produced by radioactive elements, subatomic processes (such as the annihilation of an electron-positron pair), or very violent astrophysical phenomena. Because of the great amount of energy they release, gamma rays are a type of ionizing radiation capable of penetrating deeply into matter and seriously damaging the nuclei of cells. Because of this capability, gamma rays are used mostly to sterilize medical equipment and foods.

Gears

Toothed wheels that mesh or engage with each other or with a chain, transmitting rotational motion from one to another. The most common types are the rack and pinion as well as cylindrical, conical, helical, and worm gears.

Generator

Machine that changes mechanical energy into electrical energy.

Geothermal Energy

Energy released by hot water or steam rising from underground, as in geysers.

Gravitation

The mutual attraction between two objects with mass. It is one of the four fundamental forces known in nature. The effect of gravitation on a body tends to be commonly associated with weight.

Helium

Chemical element of atomic number 2 and symbol He. It has the properties of most noble gases, being inert, odorless, colorless, and monatomic. Helium has the lowest evaporation point of all chemical elements and can be solidified only by very great pressure. In some natural gas deposits, it is found in quantities great enough to exploit and is used to fill balloons and blimps and to cool superconductors; it is also used as bottled gas in deep-sea diving.

Hydraulic Motor

Motor that produces mechanical energy by converting the energy present in a liquid.

Hydraulic Pump

Device that takes advantage of the kinetic energy of water to move part of the liquid to a higher level. It can be of two types: piston or centrifugal.

Hydrogen

Chemical element with atomic number 1 and symbol H. At room temperature, it is a colorless, odorless, and flammable gas. Hydrogen is the lightest and most abundant chemical element in the universe. For most of their lifetime, stars consist primarily of hydrogen in a plasma state. Hydrogen is present in a multitude of substances, such as water and organic compounds, and it can react with most elements.

Hydrophone

Electrical transducer of sound that is used in water or other liquid, as a microphone is used in the air. Some hydrophones can also be used as emitters. Hydrophones are used by geologists and geophysicists to monitor seismic activity.

Induction

Phenomenon that produces an electromotive force (voltage) in a medium or body exposed to a changing magnetic field or in a medium moving in relation to a fixed magnetic field. When the body is a conductor, an induced current is produced. This phenomenon was discovered by Michael Faraday, who stated that the magnitude of the induced voltage was proportional to the variation of the magnetic field.

Internal-Combustion Engine

Engine in which the mixture of air and fuel (e.g., gasoline or natural gas) is ignited by an electrical spark from the spark plug.

Isotope

In general, each chemical element is made of several species of atoms of different mass or atomic weight. Each one of these species is called an isotope of the given element. The atoms of each isotope have the same atomic number as well as the same proton number (Z), but they have a different mass number (A). These properties indicate that each isotope has a different and characteristic number of neutrons. The word "isotope" comes from the Greek, meaning "in the same place," as all isotopes of the same element are classified in the same place on the periodic table. By convention, isotope names are composed of the element name followed by the mass number, separated by a hyphen—for example, carbon-14, uranium-238, and so on. If the relation between the number of protons and neutrons is not stable, the isotope is radioactive.

Joule

Unit of energy and work defined as the work realized by a force of 1 newton over 1 m. It is equivalent to about 0.001 Btu (British thermal unit), and it is also equal to 1 watt-second-the work done in 1 second by a potential difference of 1 volt with a current of 1 ampere.

Kinetic Energy

Energy of bodies in motion. Also called live force to differentiate it from potential energy.

Magma

Mass of molten rocks in the deepest portion of the Earth's crust caused by high pressures and temperatures and solidified through cooling. Magma can be classified into two types according to its mineral content: mafic magmas contain silicates rich in magnesium and calcium, and felsic magmas contain silicates rich in sodium and potassium.

Magnetic Declination

Name given to the variance in degrees of the magnetic North Pole from the geographic North Pole.

Natural Gas

Gas with great caloric power, made of light hydrocarbons, such as methane, ethane, propane, and butane.

Neutron

Heavy subatomic particle with no electrical charge and with slightly more mass than a proton.

Newton

Unit of force defined as the force necessary to accelerate a 2-pound (1-kg) object by 1 m/s^2. Since weight is the force exerted by gravity at the surface of the Earth, the newton is also a unit of weight. Two pounds (1 kg) is 9.81 N.

Nitroglycerin

A powerful, unstable explosive that is oily, odorless, liquid, and heavier than water. When mixed with an absorbent body, it is known as dynamite. In medicine, it is used as a vasodilator in the treatment of ischemic coronary disease, acute myocardial infarction, and congestive heart failure. It is administered orally, transdermally, sublingually, or intravenously.

Nozzle

A tubular aperture. In a jet engine, the shape of the nozzle causes the escaping exhaust gases created through combustion to produce greater thrust.

Nuclear Energy

Energy produced from nuclear reactions, such as the fission of uranium or plutonium atoms.

Nuclear Fission

Fission occurs when the atomic nucleus is divided into two or more smaller nuclei; it generates several other byproducts, such as free neutrons and photons. This process results in the emission of large quantities of energy generally in the form of gamma rays. Fission can be induced through several methods, including the bombardment of a fissile atom with another particle of appropriate energy—generally a free neutron. The particle is absorbed by the nucleus, making it unstable. The process generates much more energy than would be released in a chemical reaction. This energy is emitted in kinetic form that comes from nuclear division and other byproducts of this division. It is also emitted as gamma rays.

Polyurethane

Polyurethane is a plastic material used in the formation of many high-performance synthetic paints, such as car paints and floor stains, as well as in foams and elastic materials.

Propane

Propane is a colorless, odorless gas. It is an aliphatic hydrocarbon (alkanes). Its chemical formula is C_3H_8. Propane is mainly used as fuel. In the chemical industry, it is used during the synthesis of propylene. It is also used as a refrigerant gas and as an aerosol propellant.

Propulsion

Motion given to a body when a force acts on it. It is also the displacement of a body in a fluid, especially in the cases of self-propulsion in space.

Proton

Subatomic particle with a positive electrical charge and 1,836 times the mass of an electron. Some theories of particle physics suggest that protons can decay despite being very stable, with a half-life of at least 1,035 years. The proton and neutron together are known as nucleons, since they make up the nuclei of atoms.

Resistivity

Specific resistance of a material in opposing the flow of electrical current at a given temperature. It is the inverse of conductivity.

Shroud

In sailing, each one of the standing riggings that lends support to the top of a pole or mast and joins it to the sides or the lower masts of the boat.

Solar Cell

Photovoltaic cell that transforms solar radiation into electrical energy.

Solar Energy

Energy obtained from the Sun. It is a renewable energy source, both as a direct source of heat and as a source of light to produce electricity by using photovoltaic cells.

Thermodynamics

The branch of physics that studies energy and its transformations between its various manifestations (such as heat), as well as its capacity to do work. It is intimately related to statistical mechanics, from which numerous thermodynamic relations are derived. Thermodynamics studies physical systems at the macroscopic level, whereas statistical mechanics tends to describe them at the microscopic level.

Thermohaline Circulation

In physical oceanography, the name given to the convective circulation that globally affects the oceanic water masses. It helps transfer heat from the tropics to the poles.

Turbine

Machine that transforms the energy contained in a stream of fluid into mechanical or electrical energy.

Vacuum Pump

Compressor used to remove air and uncondensed gases from a space, thereby reducing its pressure to below atmospheric pressure.

Vibrational Motion

Periodic, oscillatory motion in which an object moves about a point of equilibrium.

Volt

The potential difference along the length of a conductor when a 1-ampere current uses 1 watt of power. It can also be defined as the potential difference existing between two points, such that 1 joule of work is necessary to move a 1 coulomb charge from one to the other.

Water Turbine

Turbine that directly takes advantage of the energy contained in moving water.

Watt

Unit of power equivalent to 1 joule per second. Expressed in electrical units, it is the power produced by a potential difference of 1 volt and an electrical current of 1 ampere.

Wave Motion

Motion where the disturbance of a point within a medium is distributed to other points within that medium with a net transfer of energy but not of matter.

Winch

Mechanical device, driven manually or electrically, used to lift and move heavy loads. It consists of a rotating roller around which a cable or rope is wound, exerting force on the load tied to the other end. In manual winches, crossed bars at the ends of the rotating cylinder permit the application of the necessary force. Winches are an integral part of nautical equipment, among other things.

Wind Energy

Energy obtained by converting the wind's kinetic energy into mechanical energy by rotating an axle to operate a machine or an electrical generator.

Zeppelin

Rigid airship with internal gas cells. It is named after its creator, Ferdinand von Zeppelin. Zeppelins were used in World War I.

Index